KU-517-774

Risk

Current Titles

Concepts in the Social Sciences

Risk

Roy Boyne

Open University Press
Buckingham · Philadelphia

Open University Press
Celtic Court
22 Ballmoor
Buckingham
MK18 1XW

email: enquiries@openup.co.uk
world wide web: www.openup.co.uk

and
325 Chestnut Street
Philadelphia, PA 19106, USA

First Published 2003

A catalogue record of this book is available from the British Library

ISBN 0 335 20829 0 (pb)   0 335 20830 4 (hb)

Library of Congress Cataloging-in-Publication Data
Boyne, Roy
    Risk/Roy Boyne.
        p. cm. — (Concepts in the social sciences)
    Includes bibliographical references and index.
    ISBN 0-335-20830-4 – ISBN 0-335-20829-0 (pbk.)
    1. Risk. I. Title II. Series
    HB615.B688 2003
    338.5—dc21   2002074915

Typeset by Type Study, Scarborough
Printed in Great Britain by St Edmundsbury Press, Bury St Edmunds

For Christopher and Clare

Contents

Acknowledgements

I am grateful to Adrian Darnell and Geoff Hodgson, who shared with me some of the profundities of economic science and game theory. Harold Evans found time to provide advice about the practice of investigative journalism and the world of media moguls today. David Kleinman gave me some insight into the world of cognitive psychology. Ulrich Beck's work has been a source of inspiration and I am grateful to him for the conversations we have had over the last couple of years. Fred d'Agostino gave me the benefit of his thinking on experts and expertise. Scott Lash and Sue Scott have been stimulating interlocutors on the subject of risk on many occasions. I also have to thank about three hundred undergraduate students of sociology, who took my course on the subject of risk at the University of Durham over the last five years. My colleagues at the University of Durham, Stockton Campus, were superbly supportive as I struggled to juggle various duties while finishing the manuscript. My wife, Nicola, provided the environment which made the writing both possible and worthwhile.

The Limits
of Calculation

Even when we start with naked self-interest, there are still veils. Human beings, whether or not acting as diligent agents of some corporate entity, perceive the world through a complex filter. At a minimum, language, belief and authenticated knowledge will intervene between individuals and the world that surrounds them. Describing the precise structure of that intervening lamination is a hard thing to do. Language, culture and knowledge are bonded together. They overlap and interweave. Intent examination of them reveals large areas of complexity and uncertainty. We must recognize that they are there, but often have to remain at the level of perception, especially when we face what we take to be 'objective' risk.[1]

For historical sociologist Charles Tilly (1992), the factors that condition the perception of objective risk are epistemological, vectoral and informational. This gives a more detailed account of the filters of language, culture and knowledge. The epistemological factor may be exemplified by thinking of the differences of language that lawyers, cognitive psychologists and psychiatric social workers might bring to a case in which a particular child might be at risk. Next, it is questions of culture that must be asked to get a sense of why this particular area rather than another comes under examination as a site of risk; as Max Weber (1949: 61) noted, the recognition of the existence of a problem 'coincides, personally, with the possession of specifically oriented motives and values'. As for knowledge, Tilly notes the importance of the quality of information: Is it, to use the language of the economists, perfect or imperfect in this case? Do we know everything or must we guess?

Confrontation with 'objective risk' happens to all of us: road accidents when we drive; food poisoning when we eat; financial loss when we invest; colds, influenza and worse when we gather together in groups. We avoid many of the risks to which we are subject by simply taking care: looking both ways before crossing the road; discarding food that is past its sell-by date; getting a tetanus injection after a nasty cut. These are simple cases, where there is no immediate confusion of perspective, our personal interests are focused and the information we have is good, although probably not perfect. They are also cases where the risk is primarily to ourselves, risk that can often be dealt with through our own actions. They are 'limit' cases of some socio-psychological importance because they define for us a misleadingly simple ideal state that we perhaps think ought to obtain in all circumstances. The normal context of risk analysis is, however, more complex.

This increase of complexity can take place in at least six dimensions:

1 We may not have perfect information with which to assess the risks of meat-eating or share-dealing, waste-burial or sunbathing.
2 We may be faced with risks which will not merely affect ourselves, but which will potentially impact upon others, even beyond the company for which we work or the family of which we are part.
3 We may be dealing with risk as an agent acting on behalf of others: a manager of a petrochemical plant or a teacher taking a class of schoolchildren to the zoo.
4 We may be faced with multiple perspectives on the context in question: increased risk of disastrous pollution but decreased costs of energy, in the case of either nuclear power or the transportation of oil by supertanker.
5 Professional scientific opinion may be divided: to join or not to join a currency union, whether to build a housing development on what may or may not be a fifty-year flood plain.
6 There may be some risk perspectives relevant to what we are doing that are poorly understood: genetic modification of crops and the creation by treaty of new nations are just two possible examples.

It may seem that we are faced with increasingly dense risk contexts. How can we think, social-scientifically, about these contexts and the decisions that are made, or avoided, million upon million of them, in these situations? Let us begin with the various attempts to calculate risk in a disciplined, methodologically consistent kind of way.

There are three approaches to the calculation of risk:

1 The expression of all possible outcomes in terms of their probabilities.
2 The expression of particular future outcomes in terms of their statistical likelihood based on what has happened in lots of similar cases in the past.
3 The estimation of future events based on the widest range of experience, knowledge and care that can reasonably be expected to be applied to the context in question.

I will refer to these three approaches – knowing the odds, extrapolating from the statistics and making a responsible professional-state-of-the-art assessment – collectively as the calculative paradigm. In general, no matter what the context, it is underpinned *inter alia* by the disciplines of mathematics, statistics and the sciences – including their history of application – which cover the context in question.

Risk and uncertainty

Frank Knight, in his classic 1921 text, made a distinction between risk and uncertainty.[2] For Knight, risk is measurable. It means not knowing what will happen but knowing the probabilities of the possible outcomes. Uncertainty, on the other hand, means not knowing the probabilities of the possible outcomes, or, indeed, on many occasions what all the outcomes might be. It would be convenient but impracticable to follow Knight's usage; the general diffuse meanings attached to the term 'risk' will resist the successful imposition of precise definition. Nevertheless, we must clearly understand and retain the sense of the distinction that Knight pointed to. Thus I will, in general, use the term 'measurable risk' to refer to what Knight meant by the term 'risk'.

Where risk can be measured, its measurement takes two forms. The first of them determines the *a priori* probability of the various outcomes. The second method of measurement is used when this is not possible. Instead, it assesses likely statistical probability by collecting and analysing information about previous events, and then extends the past statistical trend into the future to arrive at a predictive judgement. How much should the life assurance company charge me for the policy I take out to cover my new mortgage? They need to know how likely I am to die. Since they are asked to make hundreds of these judgements every week, they use statistical trends to arrive at pretty accurate decisions about how much to charge. If neither *a priori* nor statistical measurement of risk is possible, we are forced to resort to, what Knight called, 'estimates'. In the everyday worlds of organizations and individuals, most analyses of risk are estimates. They are, in Knight's thinking, judgements in the context of uncertainty. I will refer to such judgements, when they are arrived at in an appropriately careful manner, as 'estimated risk'.

The basis of *a priori* risk measurement is mathematical. The roulette player knows that a wager on a single number, if the wheel has one zero, has one chance in thirty-seven of succeeding. The best poker players will know, when waiting for the last card to be dealt face-up, what the odds are for the card they want appearing. *A priori* risk measurement operates within a closed universe. In a game of Russian roulette with a six-shooter, there is one chance in six that the next player to pull the trigger will die. If Russian roulette, unknowingly, is played with a semi-automatic pistol, which loads a bullet from any of its chambers, the result is certain, and was the outcome for a man in Houston on 24 February 2000. Career gamblers, of course, do not play Russian roulette, at least not if they want long careers. Professional poker or bridge players know *a priori* what the odds are, all other things being equal, for the emergence at a given point of a particular card. They also know *a priori* that over time, and therefore the multiplication of such eventualities, again all other things being equal, the actual fall of the cards is going to correspond, increasingly closely, to a confirmation of the mathematical probability.[3] In a poker game with thirty-six cards unknown, four spades in my hand and no others showing, I know I have a one in four chance of completing my flush as the last card is dealt to me, and I can bet accordingly. I also know that over time I am going to make that flush or straight, or whatever it is, roughly in line with the odds.

These are practical expressions of a general faith in the 'law of large numbers' first advanced by Jacques Bernoulli in 1713. The essence of this proposed law was that over the long run actual outcomes would more or less conform to *a priori* probabilities. As Knight (1921: 46) put it, 'results become predictable in accordance with the laws of chance, and the error in such prediction approaches zero as the number of cases is increased'. Now, if I look back over my (almost hypothetical) career as a poker player and find that, despite my playing according to the *a priori* probabilities, I have lost much more often than I would have expected, then I can assume that other factors have intervened. I have been playing in a crooked game; I am giving away what I hold in my hand because of mannerism or expression; I am reading the odds correctly but not deducing correctly how much I should be betting; the other players are inferring more from the cards than I am and so are making better judgements of the probabilities; I am making mistakes and losing concentration; I am drawing wrong inferences from the way that the other players are betting; and so on. What it probably amounts to is that I am not a good poker player, since there is more to poker than simply knowing the odds.

Beyond this brief demonstration that the successful negotiation of even the most stripped-down *a priori* mathematically analysable risk context requires complex non-numerical skills and quality of judgement, there is an additional reason to doubt that the search for *a priori* mathematical certainty is the single key to optimal risk-decision-making. It relates to the question of prudence. What became known as the St. Petersburg problem was published in 1713 (Gigerenzer *et al*. 1989: 14–17). Consider the following coin-tossing game. You are 'heads'. On the first toss of the coin, if it is 'heads', you receive £2 and the game is over. On the second toss of the game, if it is 'heads' you receive £4 and the game is over. On the third toss £8, on the fourth toss £16, and so on. The end of the game arrives with the first time the coin falls 'heads'. What is a fair price to play this game? In the eighteenth century, it was thought it could be worked out *a priori* very simply: you wager £1 to win £2 on the first throw, another £1 to win £4 on the second throw, another £1 to win £8 on the third throw, and so on. Since it is conceivable that there might be an infinite run of 'tails', a fair price for playing the game would be infinitely high.[4] This defied common sense to such an extent that it set off a whole literature and produced fundamental change in the mathematical theory of probabilistic expectation. Nicholas Bernoulli, who first formulated the St. Petersburg problem, was a rationalist committed to the ideal of the *a priori*; his cousin Daniel, reflecting the increasing contemporary importance of the mercantile worldview, thought prudence to be a necessary component of risk assessment. As Gigerenzer *et al*. (1989: 15) put it: 'The prototypical reasonable man was no longer an impartial

judge but rather a canny merchant, and the mathematical theory of
probability reflected that shift.'

It might, at first sight, be thought attractive to base an understanding of risk on completely non-cultural principles of mathematical certainty. But, as we can glean from the St. Petersburg
problem, the post-Enlightenment history of *a priori* mathematical
thinking indicates that the idea of a *mathesis universalis* – belief in
an incorrigible mathematical logic ruling everything and awaiting
discovery at every point, which might, for example, be drawn from
the work of Descartes and Leibniz – was being questioned by the
middle of the eighteenth century.[5] What we can be clear about now
is that there is no single purely mathematical route to the essence
of risk. In even the simplest of cases, rationality and culture will
mutually inform and deform each other.

The development of statistical risk analysis seems to present an
equally complex picture. Mortality rates have been estimated since
1662 and the first scheme for annuities (annuity holders invest a
lump sum and get an annual payment for the rest of their lives) was
put forward in Holland less than ten years later, but the latter years
of the seventeenth century saw virtually no development in the
drawing of rigorous conclusions from the analysis of the past. The
field of insurance grew in importance throughout the eighteenth
century, yet was largely deaf to advances in statistics and probability. Lorraine Daston (1987) explains that insurers applied their
long experience to individual cases, and remained focused on the
individual variations that the mathematicians found irrelevant
because they cancelled out in the long run. Eighteenth-century life
insurance contracts were, then, mostly underwritten on the basis of
a practical rationality drawn from experience rather than rigorous
extrapolation from *post factum* quantification. There was, however,
substantial change as the nineteenth century opened. The first
United States census was taken in 1790 and the official statistics
office of Prussia opened in 1805 – and that was fifteen years after
the establishment of the French Bureau of Political Arithmetic.

Dissociation from the hegemonic narratives of experience and a
possible pointer to new orders of judgement can be found in the
1806 memorandum of Emile Duvillard, who had been director of
the French Bureau. He wrote:

> Facts all have essential and necessary relationships with one another.
> The same causes that modify some, also introduce differences into the
> others ... one can often represent their relationships and laws by

means of equations ... There are important facts it will always be difficult to know completely through observation. Examples would be: the duration of marriages, or widowhood; the inventory of stocks and shares, of industrial products, of raw and worked materials ... facts ... with details and on whose accuracy one can rely, may be expounded in tables. This form, which displays the facts, facilitates comparisons ... to this end, one should keep records ... rough estimates ... are ... not enough.

(cited in Desrosières 1998: 37–9)

The advocacy of rigorous recording, from Duvillard and countless others, was selectively heeded throughout the nineteenth century and beyond. The actuary became a figure of considerable symbolic power, assessing risks and probabilities based on the careful analysis of past events. The Institute of Actuaries was founded in England in 1848, as a new generation of life assurance companies was being established.

There were, however, some limitations on their area of competence. Irving Pfeffer (1956) pointed out that actuarial tables did not exist for most insurance risks, and hence that the prestige of the actuary in the field of risk is overstated, with underwriters continuing to draw upon experience and established rule-of-thumb wisdom. To give a specific example, Pfeffer seems to be asking how can Bernoulli's theorem help in deciding what premium to charge for a marine all-risks policy for a supertanker? The response from Gigerenzer *et al.* to such questions is a little misleading. They imply that statistics are of no help in cases of unprecedented disaster – *Torrey Canyon* (1967) or Bhopal (1984), for example. What statistics can do, however, is help to determine the limits of cover that can be offered, indicate the points at which risk reinsurance[6] should be arranged, calculate maximum exposure across a range of risk insurance, and thereby indicate risks to the insurance company and even the whole insurance industry. It is true that risk analysis in fields such as life or motor insurance can draw on many cases to determine appropriate premiums, and it is also true that there are fewer data available for chemical complexes. In both cases, however, non-statistical information will play a key role in risk assessment: the general insurance record of the chemical company, the experience of comparable plants elsewhere. Here the risk may not always be clearly measurable, but it can be carefully estimated. In the case of life assurance decisions, we are usually dealing with measurable risk, but not always. The current development of the

insurance industry's response to genetic testing is an indicator of
that, the addition of new factors moving decision-making from the
realm of measurement into that of estimation (until such a point
that a statistical history of the new factors can be brought to bear).
The difficulty here is, of course, that with the current rate of technological and environmental change, one is often, if not always,
dealing with shifting variables that are not easy to take full account
of through actuarial approaches. Conversely, in cases where there
are no tables, where even a disciple of Duvillard would founder, the
rational approach is to do whatever can be done to incorporate the
risk under consideration into a class of risks for which something is
known. In 'casino capitalism', to use Susan Strange's (1986) phrase,
tabulation may often not be sufficient, but some form of disciplined
approach to risk estimation is crucial.

Elaborating his concept of the *estimate*, Knight thought as
follows:

> A manufacturer is considering the advisability of making a large
> commitment in increasing the capacity of his works. He 'figures' more
> or less on the proposition, taking account as well as possible of the
> various factors more or less susceptible of measurement, but the final
> result is an 'estimate' of the probable outcome of any proposed course
> of action. What is the 'probability' of error . . . in the judgement? It is
> manifestly meaningless to speak of either calculating such a proba-
> bility *a priori* or of determining it empirically by studying a large
> number of instances. The essential and outstanding fact is that the
> instance in question is so entirely unique that there are no others . . .
> like it to form a basis for any inference of value about any real proba-
> bility in the case we are interested in. The same obviously applies to
> the most of conduct and not to business decisions alone.
>
> (Knight 1921: 226)

As Knight points out, judgements are made continuously. Not only
that, judgements are made as to the probable reliability of the
judgements. 'The business man himself not merely forms the best
estimate he can of the outcome of his actions, but he is likely also to
estimate the probability that his estimate is correct'. There are,
then, two levels of risk judgement here: that on the proposed action
and that on the level of confidence in that risk analysis. In Knight's
language, we have 'the formation of an estimate and the estimation
of its value' (p. 227).

Confidence levels with respect to risk analyses are crucial.
Certain individuals and organizations may gain a history of making

sound decisions. General knowledge of such a history will be valuable in helping to assess the probable success of future decisions. This extra thrust can be factored into the decision-making process, perhaps making decisions that would have been previously marginal into decisions in which one can now have confidence. The decision as to where to locate this margin is the third level of judgement in which we must be interested. We must add it to the two that Knight gave us, so that we now have

- the formation of estimative judgement,
- the estimation of the value of that judgement,
- the estimation of the effect of that valuation.

Knight had already pointed to this, saying, 'men do form, on the basis of experience, more or less valid opinions as to their own capacity to form correct judgements, and even of the capacities of other men in this regard ... this capacity for forming correct judgements is the principal fact which makes a man serviceable in business' (p. 229).

Within the calculative paradigm, however, the key level is the first one: What is the range of experience, knowledge and care that has been be applied to the context in question? In other words, has the estimated risk been arrived at in a disciplined way? If the answer to that question is negative, then we are outside the calculative paradigm. Knight comments in general as follows:

> ... mathematical or *a priori* ... probability is practically never met with in business ... It is difficult to think of a business 'hazard' with regard to which it is in any degree possible to calculate in advance the proportion of distribution among the different possible outcomes. This must be dealt with, if at all, by tabulating the results of experience ... It is evident that a great many hazards can be reduced to a fair degree of certainty by statistical grouping – also that an equally important category cannot.
>
> (Knight 1921: 215)

When on the territory defined by those hazards that cannot be statistically grouped, we will need to know, in the analysis of any given case, whether these hazards have been approached in a disciplined way.

Let us recap and move forward. The opening distinction, in our effort to describe and evaluate the treatment of risk within the social sciences, is between a mathematically disciplined approach to future possibilities, which is applied to measurable risks, and risks that cannot be measured but only estimated. With measurable risk, we know the odds, but we do not know the specific outcomes. These are limit cases that are illuminated by case studies in gambling and life assurance. They are not paradigmatic for understanding the culture of risk assessment in the twenty-first century. Knight was quite right to say that most decisions are set in the context of uncertainty, but he did not make the crucial distinction between uncertainty in the context of its disciplined (in the sense of the reasonable use of all available resources – scientific, mathematical, experiential and political-economic) reduction and uncertainties where that effort of reduction is compromised or even absent.[7] Only in the former case can we properly speak of estimated risk.

The normal management of measurable and estimated risk

The general strategies of risk management within the calculative paradigm are aggregation and specialization. Aggregation involves bringing together groups of cases and circumstances and, therefore, dealing with the group and not the individual case. This is a founding principle of insurance. Insurance companies spread risk and reduce uncertainty by dealing with large numbers of cases. The cases do not even need, at the limit, to be entirely similar. As Knight (1921) rather loosely noted, 'the mere fact that judgement is being exercised in regard to the situations forms a fairly valid basis for assimilating them into groups' (p. 251). The insurance of a footballer's feet, a concert pianist's hands and a perfumier's nose may be dealt with by the same underwriter. We are not, however, just talking about insurance here. The principle of spreading risk also applies to running an organization. If the scale of operations can be extended, this can increase the number of judgements made and decisions taken, resulting, at least in Knight's perception, in 'a greater probability that bad guesses will be offset by good ones, and that a degree of constancy and dependability in the total results will be achieved' (p. 252). The same principle applies in managing an individual share portfolio: increasing the number of investments made will mean that, *ceteris paribus*, variations from expected patterns will tend to cover each other with the result being a higher degree of predictability.[8]

Specialization is a rational outcome of the management of risk by aggregation. Bringing together similar cases allows for the development of expertise. What is less obvious, however, is that the process allows and even requires the emergence of categories of specialized risk-takers. As Knight puts it, 'the most important instrument in modern economic society for the specialisation of uncertainty, after the institution of free enterprise itself, is *speculation*' (p. 255). Second, and Knight has nothing to say on this aspect of the matter, the arrival of expert risk-takers leads to changes in the cultural understanding of risk. If there are more risk-takers and more forms of risk-taking, the world will come to seem a riskier place than it used to be, even if the apparent proliferation of risk-taking is due to disciplined attempts to reduce risk overall. We will look at this aspect in the next two chapters, but here we need to explain the relationship between risk management and speculation.

This, at first sight, is counter-intuitive, that speculation could be a strategy for the management of risk and the reduction of uncertainty, but a manufacturer or an importer wishing not to be exposed to the risk of fluctuating raw material prices is enabled to purchase an option to buy at a future time and at a set price due to the existence of futures markets, the essence of which is speculation on prices going up and down. What from one perspective appears to be an increase in risk – the arrival of various forms of speculation – is from another perspective a matter of the reduction of uncertainty. A further significant benefit of this field of speculation is the emergence of 'knowledge workers', whose activities not only service the speculators, but also feed into the prior decisions by manufacturers, exporters, importers and others, whose information provision is that much closer (although still a distance away in most cases) to 'perfect'.

The division of labour within organizations can also, in part, be understood in terms of aggregation and specialization. Dividing the sales function from the manufacturing function from the accounting function from the research and development (R&D) function enables different bodies of expertise to be built up, but also insulates to some extent the stable arenas of accounting and manufacturing process from the more volatile areas of marketing and R&D: this is aggregation and specialization in the same breath. For Knight, overall:

> The relation between management which consists in making decisions, and taking the consequences of decisions, which is the most fundamental form of risk-taking in industry, will be found to be a very

intricate as well as intimate one ... it is fundamental to the entrepreneur system that it tends to promote better management in
addition to consolidating risks and throwing them into the hands of
those most disposed to assume them.

(Knight 1921: 260)

The source of this 'better management' is the autonomous expertise that the processes of aggregation and specialization inevitably
create. Knight did not fully appreciate, at the time of his writing in
1921, that management itself would have to develop as a field of
expertise autonomous from, but overarching, the separate fields of
specialization created by 'rational' risk management. So he did not
anticipate the part that 'management' would play in arbitrating
different risk assessments within the same organization, an issue
that was, for example, right at the core of the *Challenger* disaster in
1986, and which is of critical importance for understanding risk
today. The signs were there, however, and Knight's identification
of the entrepreneurial role as central in the economics of risk is a
helpful starting point.

The blinkered entrepreneur

Let me be clear where we are headed. In dealing conceptually with
risk, economic actors operate within the terms of sets of possible
outcomes whose probabilities are most often impossible to predict
accurately. However, whether a set of desired outcomes is
described in terms of expected profit, anticipated job creation,
numbers of new patents, or whatever group of bounded possibilities, it is paradigmatic that the outcomes are both limited and
specified. There will be other outcomes, incidental to the achievement of the sought-for goals: a failed job interview was the final
straw and led to domestic violence; one of the new patents was
thalidomide; higher than expected profits brought the company
some prominence and it was taken over, only to be closed three
years later. Economics, the 'science' of risk-taking, cannot and does
not deal with extrinsic consequences.[9]

What Knight does is

... to isolate and define the essential characteristics of free enterprise
as a system or method of securing and directing cooperative effort in
a social group ... showing what the system is, it is hoped that advance
may be made toward discovering what such a system can and what it
cannot accomplish. A closely related aim is that of formulating the

data of the problem of economic organisation, the unchangeable
materials with which, and conditions under which, any machinery of
organisation has to work.

(Knight 1921: viii)

He defines economics here in terms of the statistics of commodities
and prices and the applied psychology of motivation. In this conception,[10] questions of social policy or long-wave macrohistorical
considerations are outside of its immediate concern. So, too, would
be questions of medium-term environmental degradation. As
Knight explains:

> . . . sacrifice of present to future necessarily means sacrifice of a fairly
> immediate, definite, predictable, and secure future for one the oppo-
> site in all these respects, and known to lie chiefly beyond the lifetime
> of the person making the choice. Economic development involves the
> *permanent* conversion of 'present goods' into income, really a large
> income for a short period into a small one in perpetuity. It is doubtful
> whether the interest in the future 'as a whole' can be considered as
> economically rational at all.

(Knight 1921: xvi–xix)

We may, then, paraphrase Knight and say that economic development can be seen as the conversion of certainty into risk. Since it
'creates' the future as risk, the argument that we should somehow
make the future more secure in a general sense is always likely to
be slipped away from if we hold the commitment to economic
development constant.

Economics, in a formal sense, is about the process of attaining
ends and not about imposing or agreeing them. It is oriented to the
framework defined by the contingent interests of the economic
actor, whether an individual, a firm or a nation-state. It is, to be
blunt, about planning and acting now within the time-frame and
economic-interest-frame of that economic subject. As Knight says
(although it should not be inferred that he was a typical mainstream
economist), 'The theory of profit developed in my book . . . rests
upon the general view of the entrepreneur or business manager as
buying productive services "now" and selling the product in the
future' (p. xxxvii).

Seen in terms of this framework, there are here two categories of
risk: those internal to the value system of the particular economic
actor concerned (for example, will there be a demand for my
product at this price?; or will my use of human fetal tissue in this
process create such controversy that I will be prevented from

continuing?) and those external to this system (such as will my success affect other companies and thereby create some reorganizations and early retirements?; or, to think back before we knew about the hole in the ozone layer, will the widespread use of aerosols pollute the air?). This distinction between risks internal to the value and knowledge system of the economic actor and risks external to this system begins to elucidate the blinkered nature of the mercantile, entrepreneurial worldview.

This was not treated as potentially pathological[11] until the first whisperings of concern at the beginning of the second half of the twentieth century and, although it is notoriously difficult to locate the beginnings of epochal shifts with one event or development, the symptomatology of economic value critique in its current form (i.e., in its post-socialist form) probably begins with concern over nuclear energy. For the elucidation of the cultural context of risk, then, it is most important to understand the forces at this boundary between internal and external risk. It is worth noting that, at the beginning of the twenty-first century, cultural conflict – whether between 'East' and 'West' or between anti-globalization activists and the state – may be seen in terms of attack and defence at this boundary.

Normally the social system works to police the boundary and keep intrinsic economic risk and extrinsic consequences apart. This is true by definition with regard to unanticipated consequences such as the arrival of variant Creuzfeld-Jakob disease in humans, possibly caused by hyperintensive farming methods. There are, though, some extrinsic consequences that we have known about for a long time, but that we accept as *more or less* necessary for a modern society: labour market changes and the devastation that they can cause for families and communities; accidents and illnesses of every kind; social tensions arising out of structural inequalities; unplanned environmental changes, such as those being currently discussed in the contexts of global warming and biodiversity. How then do we approach risk on either side of this boundary? Let us first consider intrinsic economic risk.

Some intrinsic risks are measurable, some are not. The measurable risks have largely been 'domesticated': casinos make money, insurance companies do not often fail, vaccinations save much suffering – enough, except from the standpoint of the few who are damaged, to justify a small risk. When we cannot precisely measure the risks, we are on the territory of judgement and estimation, of uncertainty. Classically, the entrepreneur gets profit in exchange for successfully bearing risks in the context of uncertainty, in those economic contexts (that is to say, relating to the production and distribution of goods, or otherwise defined relating to the creation and exploitation of market opportunities) where the risks cannot be measured precisely. If not measurable, intrinsic risk can be estimated particularly in the light of available strategies of aggregation and specialization. Thus a venture capital organization, itself a product of specialization, may aggregate risks by funding twenty bio-tech business plans, at perhaps an average of $10 million each, in the expectation, partially underpinned by the statistical performance of previous start-up businesses, that a percentage will be successful.[12] As Knight comments, 'When the technique of business organisation has reached a fairly high stage of development a known degree of uncertainty is practically no uncertainty at all, for such risks will be borne in groups large enough to reduce the uncertainty to substantially negligible proportions' (p. 47).

While entrepreneurial risk may be estimated and mitigated, it cannot be formally insured against. This is important because insurance, as a hedge against future economic loss deriving from accident or contingency, is a general response to anticipated risk, whether this is a matter of setting aside an amount for annual maintenance or paying for fire cover or an employer's liability policy.[13] Knight explains:

> ... the typical uninsurable ... business risk relates to the exercise of judgement in the making of decisions by the business man ... although such estimates tend to fall into groups within which fluctuations cancel out and hence to approach constancy and measurability, this only happens *after the fact* ... the classification or grouping can only to a limited extent be carried out by any agency outside the person himself who makes the decisions, because of the peculiarly obstinate connection of a *moral hazard* with this sort of risk.
>
> (Knight 1921: 251)

The entrepreneur must be motivated to succeed but, if insured against the risk of failure, may not be so motivated. An entrepreneur insured against the risk of failure is no longer an entrepreneur and, crucially, may no longer be motivated to estimate risks. Thus when the initiatives of huge companies are so significant for the home government(s) that *de facto* insurance provision in respect of possible failure and varieties of underperformance is in place, such organizations may be tempted or forced into decisions that they would not make under conditions in which there was no such protection. In particular, indemnification against the intrinsic risks of projects reliant upon sub-marginal infrastructure may result in the abandonment of any attempt at the disciplined estimation of risk. We may find this to have been the case, for example, with the 1984 chemical disaster in Bhopal. This concept also throws some light on decisions to build housing, towns and cities in areas that are prone to earthquakes or floods (Davis 1998).

We have now moved to the territory of extrinsic risk. Socio-environmental risk is coming to be an essential parameter within contemporary western corporate decision-making. This is a key change, since it is only relatively recently that it has become understood as central in the way that the nexus between risk and future income has been. Consider the effect in a local area of the siting of a new facility. This could be a car component plant, an incinerator or a night club. The effect on locale may, in different ways, be positive, neutral or deleterious. Knight thought that such consequences were indirect and formed 'the most important source of the need for social interference' (p. 181), and it has traditionally been the case that moving to the territory of extrinsic risk takes us away from the responsibilities of the entrepreneur and into the realm of the state, social policy and public provision:

> Many services, such as communication and education, not to mention the administration of justice, confer a general benefit on the community in addition to the special benefit to the individual, and must be encouraged by bounties or actually taken over and performed by public agencies or they will not be developed to the point of maximum benefit ... the most familiar illustrations of the opposite case in our society relate to the use of land for purposes which damage the neighbourhood, or are thought to do so ... It may be doubted whether in fact any agreement between individuals is ever made which does not affect for good or ill many persons other than the immediate parties, and a large proportion have wide ramifications over 'society'.
>
> (Knight 1921: 181–2)

It has always been the case that economic activity has led to extrinsic (unforeseen and/or incidental) advantage and disadvantage. In both cases, 'society' may step in, whether in the form of the occasional windfall tax on the supremely fortunate or by providing respite and support to those who may, for example, have lost their health due to the at first unknown carcinogenic properties of a new generation of lubricants. The intrinsic risks of social and organizational behaviour have been carried by the specific agency, whether company or individual. The extrinsic risks of such behaviour are carried by 'the society'. The dividing line between the two has been determined by foreseeability and cultural convention, and it has been generally the case that it is enshrined by law, which changes as the condition of knowledge and culture changes.

In summary, the entrepreneur's tunnel vision has been a requirement for success within the modern economy. The width of the entrepreneur's vision is a function of the economic and cultural system at the given time. Entrepreneurial action is designed to take advantage of the potential of the present shape of things in so far as it allows for a reconfiguration of the future in some small but determinate way: the launch of a new product, the provision of a more efficient service. Entrepreneurial judgement is based on the assessment of how things would be without the intervention compared with how things will develop if the plan is implemented. If the judgement is correct, the entrepreneur will be the first to arrive at this future and is prepared in advance to take advantage of the demands that will define this part of the future. Present investment risks are taken in anticipation of future gains. It is a system that is supported by law and culture in the modern world. However, for the entrepreneur, not only is the view forward a restricted one, the anticipation of its implementation even within this restricted view is almost always partial. We cannot predict the complete inventory of the consequences of actions, or exactly design those actions so that they duplicate perfectly in reality what was planned in the abstract. When these intrinsic imprecisions turn out to be major sources of failure – there never was much of a market for this product, the process did not work – this will be taken as the culpable responsibility of the entrepreneur. It will be a sign that the estimation of the risk or the subsequent quality of the decisions taken arising from that estimation were inadequate. When dealing with the disciplined estimation of intrinsic risk, there is no such thing as bad luck. This may not be the case with respect to extrinsic factors, but the boundary between intrinsic and extrinsic is dynamic.

Bhopal 1984: a case study in tunnelled visions

Union Carbide synthesized carbaryl in 1953. It is a widely effective, biodegradable insecticide with low toxicity for humans. By 1959, it was being used around the world. Eighty thousand metric tons of it

were being manufactured annually in the United States alone in the
1980s. It remains the dominant insecticide used in the agricultural
sector (Baylor 1996). In 1975, Union Carbide, having obtained a
licence to manufacture pesticides in India, established a chemical
plant to make carbaryl insecticide in Bhopal, the state capital of
Madhya Pradesh and a growing but poorly serviced industrial,
bureaucratic and agricultural centre of around half a million people
(Shrivastava 1992: 47–51). Most of the chemicals that are combined
to make carbaryl are toxic: chlorine, phosgene, carbon monoxide
and methyl isocyanate (MIC). The latter was widely used in the
manufacture of carbaryl by 1978, and it was imported in relatively
small quantities into Bhopal.

By the early 1980s, it had become clear that the Indian and neighbouring markets for pesticides were unstable. They were affected
by dramatic, often monsoon-related, annual variations in crop size,
leading to frequent withdrawal by purchasers from the market.
Uncoordinated application of pest-control led to ineffectiveness
because the insects would survive in untreated neighbouring fields
and soon return, while brand loyalty was also compromised
because farm labour did not get the training to make the best use
of the product. Strong competition among different brands, for
what insecticide business there was, restricted market share. Union
Carbide reacted to these difficulties by planning to make their
Bhopal plant more economically viable. They proposed 'backward
integration', the manufacture on site of some of the component
material used to make carbaryl. This was going to make the facility more complex and more hazardous, and the city authorities
objected, but were overruled at both state and national level: Union
Carbide India were one of the biggest employers, paying well, and
it was important to embrace the modern industrial project.

There is disagreement about what precisely happened on 3
December 1984. It is likely that many gallons of water were introduced into a tank containing tons of methyl isocyanate. Although
it was claimed by Jackson Browning, the vice-president responsible
for the health, safety and environmental programmes at Union
Carbide, that the introduction of water was malicious, it was most
likely accidental. The plant was like an old car. It generally worked,
but there were leaks and groans, with unreliable instrumentation,
corroded pipework, poorly trained operatives, regular breakdowns
and the occasional serious accident. The MIC, which boils at 38° C,
was not refrigerated as it should have been and it reacted violently

with the water. The gases caused by the reaction could have been neutralized by a caustic soda shower, but the scrubber meant to do this was out of action. Next, the gases could have been burnt off, but the flare tower was not functioning. As poison gas vented into the atmosphere at high pressure, the alarm system was inadequate to warn the local population, who in any event had not been informed about the potential dangers of the plant and were not prepared for such an emergency. This gas was heavier than air and it settled over the shanty dwellings next to the plant, eventually killing more than 2000 people and causing significant and lasting harm to perhaps a hundred times more.

Rajiv Gandhi was Prime Minister of India, and the Chief Minister of Madhya Pradesh was Arjun Singh. There is little direct evidence to indicate the attitude of these senior political figures to risk prevention. Indira Gandhi's policy of Indian industrialization was continued by her son, Rajiv, and this ideological direction was generally maintained at regional level by politicians like Arjun Singh (still, in 2002, a leading figure in Madhya Pradesh politics), who was blamed, in the State Assembly by government official Babu Lal Gour, for the proliferation of slums around the Carbide plant. On the whole, and ignoring the inevitable flak, political leaders are mandated to uphold constitutions, to follow and develop the rule of law, to advance the interests of their countries and regions, and to represent their constituents in whatever wider forum.

The diversification of Union Carbide India Ltd (UCIL) into chemical and plastics in the 1960s would have been seen as desirable. The low rent charged for the UCIL plant in Bhopal was a sign that they were welcome. Although the slightly inferior specification of the Bhopal plant compared with the one in Institute, West Virginia (Bhargava 1986: 7–11), hints that the visitors might not have been all that they seemed, surely no one doubted that Union Carbide 'expected to contribute to – and benefit from – growing national economies around the world' (Browning 1993: 2). As Weber (1947) put it, 'All economic activity in a market economy is undertaken and carried through by individuals [or corporate groups] to make provision for their own ideal or material interests' (p. 319). No doubt industrial society is a more acutely dangerous place, at least for a few unfortunate people who are involved in accidents of various sorts, but the benefits of increased prosperity, such as reduced deaths from starvation and disease, were thought to outweigh massively such costs. In addition, in this case – and not untypically – Union Carbide were seen as world experts, with safety standards that would in part define the norm. In these terms, the location of the plant in Bhopal would not have been seen as irresponsible. There are, however, further elements here. India achieved independence in 1947. It is a post-colonial society and, since the 1980s, a nuclear power. It can quite properly expect its own people to be trained and developed to operate a plant such as the one in Bhopal: it would have been politically, economically and culturally unacceptable to embrace a pure industrial colonialism. However, there was not the wealth to resource a state-of-the-art programme of training and management transfer (nor even anything approaching an adequate system of factory inspection) (Shrivastava 1992: 25). The Indian government would not have had the mandate to single this plant out for special treatment, and Union Carbide's responsibilities to their shareholders would have precluded deliberately and 'unnecessarily' increasing the losses on their Bhopal investment.

Union Carbide Corporation (UCC) were led by their chairman, Warren Anderson; the principal actors at UCIL (50.9 per cent owned by UCC) were chairman Keshub Mahindra, managing director Vijay Gokhale and works manager J. Mukund.[14] All, together with Browning and a few others, are still, eighteen years after the event, subject to civil and criminal actions in the Indian courts. Of these, only Mukund had any 'on the ground' responsibility, but his reported response to a state-level inquiry following an earlier MIC discharge, that the leak could not possibly have come from his plant, ought to have given Arjun Singh's state administration cause for concern. UCC had responded to the structural context of its Bhopal responsibility as well as it thought it could. In 1982, a team was sent to the Bhopal plant from the United States to carry out what was effectively a handover report. The remaining US engineers were due to exit, and to achieve closure their parting present was a list of the things that needed to be done at the plant. In the 1982 UCC survey, ten areas were identified as requiring urgent attention, half of which contributed to the disaster:

- the potential for toxic gases being released into the air;
- inadequate spray protection;
- problems of MIC storage integrity;
- instrumentation and safety valve failure;
- personnel turnover.

Mukund authored an action plan, but events in December 1984 showed that it had not been fully implemented and, in 1989, the Indian Supreme Court agreed to a settlement of $470 million by Union Carbide to those surviving the disaster.

How in 1982, when the last US personnel with responsibility for running the plant departed, would UCC have estimated their risk exposure? We know the answer to this question. UCIL had taken over full operational responsibility for running the plant. UCIL directors and managers had been fully briefed about the weak points in the operation. The Indian authorities had issued their various permits and licences. UCC had an 'all risks' worldwide policy covering them for $200 million in the event of anything unforeseen. They would have estimated, with all this in place, that they had fulfilled their responsibilities to their shareholders and employees. They had not entirely withdrawn, almost certainly due to a combination of political pressures and a residual hope that the Indian agri-markets would eventually become robust, meaning that UCC would be well-situated to further develop market share. But the insurance policy together with the 'closure' report would have seemed to UCC to cover the residual risk attendant upon their retained position in relation to the plant.

What, however, of the people of Bhopal? How would UCC have estimated the risks to them? There is no evidence that they asked the question, no sign that they tried to estimate the risk of this plant wiping out the whole neighbourhood. This was not something outside their value-frame. There had been previous major disasters within the industry. UCC passed operational responsibility for a creaking and groaning toxic material processing plant with ten major faults to a 'member of their own family' and, understandably, were held responsible when this huge accident occurred. We can infer that UCC did not carry out a state-of-the-art risk estimation with respect to the plant handover. We can guess that the insurance cover of $200 million, which was for UCC worldwide, not just for Bhopal, was arrived at by calculating at local levels of expected compensation where appropriate rather than US levels. We can also infer that there was a similar view taken on locally appropriate safety levels. In the final analysis, it would seem that UCC just took a risk, which is what entrepreneurs do. If, and this is debatable, the people of such places as Bhopal are now seen as stakeholders in a way that was not recognized in the early 1980s, perhaps such risks are now not quite so sanguinely taken. But it remains the case, at least in the United States, that '[u]ntil the controversy over corporate social responsibility is politically and legally resolved, the shareholder primacy conceptualization remains the prevailing legal doctrine underpinning corporate governance' (Knoke 2001: 256).

There is currently no public knowledge of Dow Chemicals' risk analysis in regard to the 1984 Bhopal event, consequent upon their purchase of UCC on 6 February 2001; how they plan to maximize their minimum gain from the acquisition of UCC is a question that future researchers may be able to answer. In the meantime, the victims of the 1984 event and their families have registered deep concern that the legal disappearance and symbolic evacuation of Union Carbide will make their struggle harder. It is possible that the risks represented by these petitioners are extrinsic to Dow's risk-analytical framework.

2
Risk in the Media

I will generally refer to mainstream broadcast journalism and accompanying editorial or features commentary as the media,[1] or, to give it a fuller title, the news media or documentary[2] media. I will not distinguish particularly between the forms through which, for example, the BBC or CNN presents information and comment, whether television, radio, print or internet. The cultural values and beliefs carried by the media are generally reflective of the widest possible (compatible with retention of the core 'customer' base) context of cultural consent for the media organization concerned – we live in the era of the imperative to maximize audiences and influence. The media do not have as a core objective the dissemination of knowledge about risks, although in their capacity as profit-making or state-sponsored organs of news and commentary broadcasting, they are a massively important organ for doing so.[3]

The language of broadcasting

The language of risk within the broadcast media is not rigorous. No consistent distinction is made between risk and uncertainty, or between measurable risk and estimated risk. Statistical information or historical antecedents will not generally be presented in any detail, although their importance may be referred to. Editors, feature writers and journalists do not usually address themselves to the task of providing support to those with professional responsibilities with respect to risks under discussion; indeed, it may often be presented as a duty to criticize them when justified. The task of apportioning responsibility, either for past events or for necessary actions in the future, may be undertaken. It may not, and because of pressures of time and resources often cannot, be discharged to the level of competence which might be required in a boardroom, a court of inquiry or a social work case study conference. The media, however, fulfil the demand for instant coverage and commentary, and so cannot aspire to the state-of-the-art multi-disciplinary investigation desirable if it is proposed, for example, to build a new runway for an existing airport or an oil pipeline between eastern Siberia and China.

The media employ directly large numbers of specialists. For example, the larger television companies have scientific correspondents, sports specialists and health spokespersons, to name but a few. These people are generally recruited from the relevant professional ranks, which does enable editorial meetings to comprise representatives from several areas. This is a recipe for a fast service that is as broad, competent and acute as the circumstances could possibly allow. So it is that the BBC and CNN, to take two leading examples, have a high reputation. There are, however, two structural features of the editorial process of multi-disciplinarity that must be borne in mind. The first is that multi-disciplinary communication requires the working out of discursive compromises between the various participants. Sometimes that may be barely noticeable as a literary critic, novelist and priest engage in a televised conversation concerning a novel set in the aftermath of Auschwitz. Sometimes this will be more difficult if a mathematical economist, a political historian and a skilled political interviewer are planning an interview with a defence secretary on the economic and social impact of an armed intervention. Additionally, many trained professionals may have very different attitudes to risks which they may regard as routine (the economist's view of bankruptcies or the Army general's view of casualties, for example) as compared with a typical view within the general public. It is the editor's job to see that such different languages and assumptions are knitted together to create a discourse accessible to the relevant audience. The second structural feature, then, is the general requirement of orienting broadcast output to the intelligent consumer. When this second feature is combined with the compromises – of language and base assumptions – required by multi-disciplinarity, then we move towards the conclusion that media discussions of risk will not generally be sufficient on which to base sound judgements. In other words, they should be treated as mere introductions. But media discussion and reportage of risks is not accompanied by any kind of health warning, and there are deeper processes at work that require excavation. To get at them, we will take a longish detour into the way that the media deal with the risks to their own organizations.

In the late 1980s, Susan Shapiro was a research fellow at the American Bar Foundation. She became interested in how newspaper editors and television producers dealt with the risk of being sued for libel. Since at least 1964, the Supreme Court had encouraged news organizations to pursue the truth, and not to withdraw from that pursuit just because of the risk of broadcasting something that might be false.[4] However, there were concomitant obligations, listed by Shapiro (1992: 132) as: 'responsibility, objectivity, even-handedness, accuracy, impartiality, fairness, balance, and credibility'. What this amounted to was that 'journalists face a tension between unknowingly printing falsehood in pursuit of free unfettered speech and practising excessive restraint in the name of . . . responsibility' (p. 132). This exercise of restraint was called, in US journalistic argot, 'chilling'. In 1991, the average size of a libel award was $2 million, and defending a libel action would significantly increase the direct costs, without taking any account yet of organizational disruption and risk to reputation. On the other side, the time, effort and money needed to mount a libel action would usually be less than the burden on defendants. The emergence of a libel-conscious society had led, Shapiro thought, to increasing self-censorship by journalists, who became more cautious, ignoring high-risk stories, avoiding stories about private individuals because their duty of care to them is greater than to public figures, and abandoning stories whose sources had to be protected. In this context, the editorial function tended to impose stricter protocols of newsroom behaviour, tightening control, getting facts double-checked for every story (Libson 2001) and, lastly, employing lawyers to confirm whether a story is 'safe' or not.

To research this environment, and establish some of the consequences of this mode of risk management by news organizations, Susan Shapiro interviewed fifty-three libel lawyers, all of whom advised newspapers and TV companies on libel risks. As she pointed out, this constituted a significant proportion of all such lawyers in the United States. Through these interviews, she was able to rationally reconstruct[5] the procedure that they all, more or less, followed, and thereafter to ruminate on some of the implications and consequences of their methods.

Shapiro found that US libel lawyers asked two basic questions when they assessed a news story: Is it potentially defamatory and has there been an invasion of privacy? The main emphasis of their work focused on the first question. Here the first thing to note is, as one respondent explained:

> Rarely is the problem in the lead. Reporters know how to check that and the central claims of the story exhaustively. It's usually several paragraphs down in the story – a story in a story or a small detail or an ancillary point. For example, you're reporting a fire and mention that an adjacent building, a bankrupt business, was also burned. Turns out the business is not bankrupt.

(Shapiro 1992: 145)

So the lawyers examine the story very carefully, looking for every detail that could be construed as unsafe. Suppose they find indication of defamation. The remaining tasks for the libel lawyer are (i) to determine if the defamation might be false and (ii) to see if there is any negligence, fault or unreasonable behaviour on the part of the journalist team. This presents a classic hermeneutic situation: 'Lawyers have not been in the field. They did not observe the events, listen to the press conferences, read the documents, hear the interviews, talk to the sources' (Shapiro 1992: 145). Nevertheless, they have to draw inferences, apply legal conventions with respect to rules of evidence and standards of proof, and try to reconstruct the process by which the journalist came to present the story as news.

In working through the information given to her by the fifty-three lawyers, Susan Shapiro found nine themes in the work they did.

1 The search for 'give-aways' suggesting the journalist is unsure – terms like 'seems' or 'appears'; perhaps a central part of the story buried towards the end indicating a lack of confidence in its truth.
2 A check for incongruous verbal fireworks.
3 A concern for consistency and the coherence of the story, such as whether the opening statements match the detail.
4 Do all the parts of the piece, the words and pictures for example, hang together?
5 Are there glaring implications of the story that are untouched?
6 Where was the evidence obtained?
7 Did the journalists try to check out the other side to see if the claims within the story might be wrong?

8 Is the story placed in context, or are there elements that have been left out?
9 Has the media organization exhausted all the possibilities of substituting safe sources (like documents of public record or press releases) for the ones used?

The consequence of all this work was not that these lawyers recommended lots of stories be dropped. Shapiro found that they rarely did recommend the complete loss of a story: all but two of the fifty-three said they never gave such advice. What the lawyers did was to try to find a way to allow the journalists to say what they wanted to say at the same time as giving them maximum legal protection. This means, importantly, two things: removing items from the periphery of the story and relying on safe sources. There are two very significant consequences of this. Shapiro puts the first of them as follows:

> [On the] advice that reference to secondary characters be excised. The effect is to narrow stories, to conceal the complex social networks and inter-organizational relationships that figure in collective action . . . The reluctance to name these ancillary contributors to newsworthy events creates a simplistic (mis)understanding of social behaviour by a citizenry whose formal education in the social sciences often comes from its exposure to the press.
>
> (Shapiro 1992: 156)

The second consequence to be highlighted derives from the pressure to use safe sources; in other words, to use public records, governmental agency pronouncements, company press briefings. This means that there may be a tendency for the press to use official definitions of risk situations and that there may be important stories that do not get told, perhaps mostly because the official versions of them remain too skeletal to be newsworthy.

Shapiro's valuable and under-recognized work strengthens the case for arguing that media presentation of risk must be seen as, at best, introductory. There is, however, a further twist that we must examine. Thus far we have proceeded as if the world is a clear if sometimes difficult text that media workers read and then re-present, but, as Harold Evans (1998: 7) put it, 'the "mirror" concept is no guide to an editor'.

Consider the following exchange reported by Simon Hattenstone (1998):

Last week I received a phone call from Fox . . . In that day's *Friday Review* there was a small article about Betty Thomas, the director of Dr. Doolittle . . . 'Hello Simon', said my friendly public relations woman. 'About the Betty Thomas piece, it wasn't very *keen,* was it? . . . [I]t wasn't very *positive*'. 'Ah', I said. Had anyone asked her to tell us that the piece was insufficiently keen? 'Yes, I had a phone call from America, and they wanted us to tell you that they're not happy with the piece. They say that in future, *if there is to be a future* . . .' . . . I use this conversation to illustrate an alarming trend . . . While more and more space is being devoted to movies in the press, journalists are being allowed less and less access. The studios are eager, desperate even, for the column inches, but they want to control what is written.

For the media, fear of being sued may pale into insignificance when compared with the risks of being kept out of the loop. Nothing will be more important for media organizations than preserving access to 'the news'. One way of dealing with the threat of exclusion is to make sure that the media organization is itself thoroughly a part of the world that is being reported on. Out of which it will come as no surprise that one commentator, Ben Bagdikian, has openly suggested that 'the behaviour of the new corporate controllers of public information has produced a higher level of manipulation of news to pursue the owner's other financial and political goals' (cited in Armao 2000). The phenomenon commented upon in *Citizen Kane*, and reproduced in the careers of Rupert Murdoch, Conrad Black and all the other powerful and tentacular media moguls, is a part of what the media are and do. The extreme case is Silvio Berlusconi, at the time of writing, prime minister of Italy. Rory Carroll (2002) takes us inside the experienced structure of saturated information in 2002 Italy as follows:

> Over breakfast you catch the news headlines on a television network owned by the prime minister. On the way to work you read a newspaper owned by the prime minister. At the office you log onto the net using a provider owned by the prime minister. At lunch you flick through a magazine owned by the prime minister. On the way home you rent a video from a chain owned by the prime minister. The film was made by a company owned by the prime minister. When it ends you channel hop, one, two, three channels, owned by the prime minister. In bed you read a book published by a company owned by the prime minister.

Carroll's article on Berlusconi was published on 1 April. It could be an April Fool story.

Having completed this detour through the methodology of the media's own risk-avoidance strategies, we have a very dark and somewhat overstated picture. It will be mitigated by codes of journalistic ethics, countless examples of professional integrity and the extensive concern for public welfare that suffuses any democracy worth its name. But it does suggest that, when the media tell the public about risks, they will do so in relatively simple terms, based on official and attributable sources, reducing access damage to their channels of support as far as reasonably possible; and that they will do all this in such a way as to maximize sales.

Cultural consent and the identification of risk

At the beginning of this century, the media remain significantly national in their editorial and operational reach (Morris and Waisbord 2001). Working to retain and even expand a national or sub-national audience, in the context of increasingly powerful supranational pressures such as US cultural power, economic unions such as the EU, or the world-level dynamics of such religious movements as Christianity and Islam, is the deep problematic for media organizations today. The situation now is entirely dissimilar to the context in which UNESCO in the 1970s opened the question of Third World dependence on First World media output, and which led to the Paris Mass Media Declaration of 1978. Even recognizing that the declaration was made in the context of Cold War politics and post-colonial struggle, it is still surprising just how dated some of its closing sentiments now seem:

> ... it is essential that bilateral and multilateral exchanges of information among all States, and in particular between those which have different economic and social systems, be encouraged and developed. ... For this declaration to be fully effective it is necessary, with due respect for the legislative and administrative provisions and the other obligations of Member States, to guarantee the existence of favourable conditions for the operation of the mass media, in conformity with the provisions of the Universal Declaration of Human Rights.
>
> (UNESCO 1978)

In the era of the Internet, the problem is not so much one of information exchange, but more of information accreditation and reliability. And, at a time when one of the regular responses to global cultural homogenization is terrorism, favourable conditions for the operation of the mass media give no guide to the negotiation of the dialectic between dumb global consumerism and strident particularism. Thus, even when Herman and McChesney (2000), who have little doubt that 'The dominant players treat the media markets as a single global market with local subdivisions' (p. 216), conclude their very helpful investigation into the global media as follows:

> We regard the primary effect of the globalization process . . . to be the implantation of the commercial model of communication, its extension to broadcasting and the 'new media', and its gradual intensification under the force of competition and bottom-line pressures. The commercial model has its own internal logic and, being privately owned and relying on advertiser support, tends to erode the public sphere and to create a 'culture of entertainment'.
>
> (Herman and McChesney 2000: 225)

We do not get a clue as to how the ideal media organization ought, in terms of general principles, to be handling either the question of knowledge authentication or that of the cultural interface between local and global. There is a lack of general, ethical public debate about what the media should inform us about (and to what standard), and about how in general the interface between local and global should be presented. So it is not surprising that much media content is spectacle and entertainment. This is a key mechanism by which the media maintain and try to expand their audience, secure in their anticipation of cultural consent to the global 'infotainment' industry. The self-marginalizing nature of resistance to this trend almost makes moderate opposition to it impossible, and the roots of this go deep into the very nature of communication itself.

Neil Postman (1986) explained things well in his polemical book, *Amusing Ourselves to Death*. His topic was the shift from the culture of print to the culture of the image, and his thesis was that critical thinking in the public sphere becomes increasingly difficult as 'television gives us a conversation in images, not words' (p. 7), explaining that while the daily news from around the world could only exist from the time of the invention of the telegraph, the emergence of television demanded that it be reformed in visual terms. This, he thought, makes careful and sophisticated public argument and exposition to a mass audience almost impossible. Modern communications technology increases the number of spectators within the public sphere; the expansion of education produces a rise in the numbers of people capable of appreciating critical argument; yet, because of the form of the dominant communications technology of our day, extended participation in nuanced public debate is rare if not unknown. This is an arresting thesis, but it rests partly on an exaggeration of the extent to which print actually did produce rational and wide public debate. It also overemphasizes the formal incapacities of television. So that when Postman says that political philosophy cannot be done on television in much the same way that it cannot be done using smoke signals – because the medium is incapable of sustaining it – he is guilty of a certain amount of hyperbole. It can be done on the television, but not so many people pay it any attention. They can be entertained on another channel. Postman's point that everything televisual must be, *ipso facto*, entertaining (p. 89) is overstated, but that every item must compete for our attention against a whole range of entertainments is surely correct.

The structural relationship between global risk communication and global entertainment is convoluted, but we can start by insisting that the global media are predominantly televisual. Global images and issues generally require placing in context for the audience: what Fairclough (1995) calls re-contextualization and others (Cohen *et al.* 1990) have referred to as domestication. Roland Robertson (1995) used the term 'glocalization' to argue that what now constitutes the local is substantially fed from the global level – we will see this absolutely basic mechanism at work in relation to environmental risk in Anderson's (1997) study of the UK press campaign about poisoned North Sea seals later in this chapter. The audience for documentary media treatments of remote events and global themes, even recontextualized, requires seduction. Emotions must be vigorously engaged or the audience will not pay the price of devoting their attention. The situation is similar to the Hollywood movie audience imperative. Adapting the work done on the media treatment of the Gulf War (Nohrstedt and Ottosen 2000) to the global risk context, the overall picture may look something like this. If the global risk theme – say radiation pollution – is directly and newly relevant to the local context, its appearance will generate emotional demands for advice, procedures and future prevention. If the theme is not directly threatening, but is affecting global friends or neighbours, we can expect a certain demand for information and, in response, a modest level of sympathetic reportage, possibly with cautionary undertones. The audience that engages with the latter will be relatively small but, as with all global communication contexts, will tend to be maximized by the documentary use of entertainment techniques – even the most serious documentary items will be edited and scripted as professionally and compellingly as time allows, with striking illustrations and the routine enhancement of whatever dramatic aspects can be demonstrated. Modelling the local reception of new, locally specific and remediable dangers is thus relatively straightforward when the story comes in from outside. If a story begins from its local area, the dynamic of any transfer to a wider level is much more uncertain. Allan Mazur's (1998a: 121–41) account of the happenstance transfer from the *Niagara Gazette* to the *New York Times* of the reportage of Love Canal[6] illustrates the uncertainties very well. As Mazur put it, 'Of numerous hazards which could be potentially the basis for a news story, few are reported at any one time ... with some relatively harmless problems receiving heavy coverage while more serious hazards are ignored' (p. 126).

Within the broadcast media, at the level of form rather than content, there are no significant differences between fact and fiction. The media presentation of risk will generally tend to the dramatic. Unavoidable competition with expensively designed and produced entertainments may force even the responsible treatment of risk by the media into pathways of emotion and spectacle. Advertising the dangers of smoking on UK television is done by filming the real tears of a daughter whose father has recently died from lung cancer. High production values and the need to hold an audience help to produce what has been called the social amplification of risk,[7] a process through which rational, self-interested speculation about the significance of trends and events may be increased in volume through the media to produce shared perceptions of great risk, general distrust and the development of local action groups (Kasperson *et al.* 2001).

Does the global televisualization of the media mean lower standards of information transmission about risk? Does the reproduction of the cultural consent of the media audience require image more than content? These questions require further research, but our earlier recognition of the structural trends towards simplification in the news now needs to be emphasized further because of the increasing dominance of the image, and due to the inevitable playing of the spectacle and exaggeration cards in the competition for audience figures in the globalizing media world.

Linked to this, Harold Evans' survey of the way that English-language newspapers have changed over the last quarter of a century implies a particular switch in the treatment of risk. In broad terms, this former path-breaking editor of the *Sunday Times* thinks that the role of newspapers as watchdogs for the public interest has been eroded as emphases have been transferred from the mode of investigative journalism to that of emotional imaging. Secured by its surrounding framework of constitutional rights, the US press may have been a model for the promotion of the general good:

> The British Press would never have been allowed to expose a British Watergate because of the laws of confidence and contempt. Conversely the American press would not have been prevented by archaic contempt of court rules from ventilating the scandal of the treatment of the thalidomide children. Even when the *Sunday Times* won the right to publish facts about the origins of the thalidomide tragedy, by a belated judgement of the European Court of Human Rights under the free speech provision of article 10, a British judge subsequently denied the newspaper the right to quote from the drug company's documents.
>
> (Evans 1998: 9)

However, Evans does not feel that this laudable US tradition has been maintained. Proliferating television news programmes have become profit centres and marketing tools, while themselves becoming underfunded[8] and forced towards repetition and audience manipulation. In this context, opinion is much easier to convey than explanation. If Evans is right to suggest that such cultural changes have taken place within the media, one would expect this to be reflected in the fortunes of investigative journalism. When we examine the work done in this area, the picture is quite confused, although it does appear that the amount of investigative journalism carried out in 1995 compared with 1980 shows a marked decline (Armao 2000: 45; Bernt and Greenwald 2000: 51–79).

Byron Acohido is an internationally known journalist who has worked for the *Seattle Times* since 1987, taking up coverage of Boeing in 1988. He says that his coverage of safety in the aerospace industry gives his readers accessible useful information and contributes to raising their already high levels of knowledge and awareness. He is able to do this because he has developed a consistent and teachable set of working practices that enable him to stay with a 'big picture' approach (Chepesiuk *et al.* 1997: 104). The pursuit of the story is the heart of it:

> I think the bulk of it is trying to develop story ideas. The Triple Seven story, I developed that over five years. I did stories all along. Like right

> now, I have a big story in mind on this 737 flaw. Weave back to the
> legal story and why. Explain the motivation, who benefits by keeping
> it unknown and stretching out the probable cause several more
> months, more than a year past the last accident . . . It seems like I'm
> always aiming toward a big story, but trying to do breaking stories. By
> the time I get to the big story, I can refer to what I broke about the
> story along the way.
>
> (Chepesiuk *et al.* 1997: 114)

Most investigative reporting is not done specifically to warn the
public of risks that they need to know about. When that happens,
it is broadly incidental to the main functional objective of getting
the story, and thus continually reproducing a general appetite for
arousing news. Marjie Lundstrom and Rochelle Sharp worked for
a Washington News agency, on infant mortality and sudden infant
death syndrome in the late 1980s. Their initial brief was just to find
a story about child abuse. What they finally produced was based on
careful analysis of mortality statistics. It was electric and produced
considerable reaction in professional circles like the Centers for
Disease Control, but was picked up by only a few newspapers.
Their work illustrated that standards of infant mortality investigation were so inconsistent across America that parents were
literally being allowed to get away with murder. Most US citizens
would not have read about it.

Chepesiuk *et al.* (1997) note that, despite the apparent importance of such work, the investigative journalists themselves are often
derided: 'People tell you that you're only after the negative, you're
such a ghoul, you're such an asshole. They get real personal, and
they make you question sometimes what you are doing' (p. 44).
During the 1990s, the contradictions inherent in the public reception of investigative journalism appeared to increase. The most
spectacular case concerned the Food Lion grocery outlets in the
United States. ABC *Prime Time Live* reporters falsified their
details to become employees, and the stores were exposed on television for recycling date-expired meat, bleaching unsafe fish and
repackaging rodent-damaged cheese. Food Lion lost millions of
dollars worth of business and sued ABC. They were initially
awarded damages of more than $5 million, for fraud and breach of
fiduciary duty. It was held that truthful information must be lawfully obtained, and that the motive for the TV programme was to
increase ratings rather than to serve the public interest (Winch
2000).

Ettema and Glasser (1998) have characterized the public appetite for inside knowledge not in terms of a rational demand for information about risk, but in terms of a desire to feel and express righteous indignation: 'The essential energy of investigative reporting is still best characterised as "righteous indignation", a term coined by Ida Tarbell a century ago as the anthem of the muckrakers' (p. 61). Of course, the rational demand for risk information can and does go together with the desire for opportunities to express righteous indignation. However, the dominance of the latter helps to explain why most investigative reporting is not primarily about risk, but about money, power, crime and politics; and the power structures of the media organizations themselves provide a clue as to why the amount of investigative reporting appears to have dropped.

Science, technology and the media

Niklas Luhmann (2000) suggested that, 'in the process of producing information, the mass media simultaneously sets up a horizon of self-generated uncertainty which has to be serviced with ever more information' (p. 11). The process of working up a story to create a demand for its next instalment is, Luhmann implies, a core feature of the media system that works

> . . . with the assumption that its own communications will be continued during the next hour or on the next day. Each programme holds the promise of another programme. It is never a matter of simply representing the world at any one given moment.
>
> (Luhmann 2000: 11)

If scientific communication is about clarifying what we do know 'at any given moment', there is a tension here. The scientific imperative is different from the media one. In the field of risk, this tension is between analysing risk and creating an appetite for its images. We can look at this in a little more detail by examining two cases in which public attention was drawn by the media to a pressure point where risk and science closely intertwine – disease. The first of these concerns the deaths of large numbers of seals washed up on the North Sea coasts of Europe in 1988. The second relates to a young woman who caught AIDS from her dentist and became a prime focus of US media attention in 1990–91.

Around springtime in 1988, there were sizeable numbers of seals dying off the British, German and Scandinavian North Sea coasts. This had come quite shortly after a similar or even larger-scale outbreak among the seals of Lake Baikal in Siberia, and may have been related to an epidemic among the crabeater seals in Antarctica in 1955. There had been a number of pollution stories in the media through the 1980s, and there was some scientific discussion about the possible linkage between the deaths of probably over 20,000 seals in the North Sea and various pollution scares. Scientific opinion shifted as the geography of the disease moved and as the symptoms varied. The candidates were pollution, herpes, picoma and canine distemper. There was the possibility of an inter-relationship with pollution poisoning, leading to reduced immunity from diseases that normally the seals might fight off. The issue of dying seals became a focal point in the Scandinavian elections in autumn 1988, with the Swedish and Danish media addressing an audience that held the North Sea to be an important source of their wealth, health and identity. British research on the problem produced inconclusive results. A seal-specific virus similar to distemper in dogs and also to measles was isolated, but there was no real breakthrough. There was, though, another pollution scare-story as a ship named the *Karin-B* was refused permission to land at Liverpool docks to unload a cargo of toxic waste.

Against this background, it appears that David English, then editor of the *Daily Mail,* decided to run a campaigning story. Alison Anderson, whose research is the prime resource here, revealed that this was a case of the media leading the way, defining a contemporary agenda, which in this particular case led very nicely to Margaret Thatcher's speech to the Royal Society on 27 September 1988, in which the then prime minister proclaimed a belief in sustainable development supported by a nurtured environment. Anderson interviewed a *Times* environmental journalist working in the field at the time, who commented as follows:

> What put it on the agenda without any question in my mind was the *Daily Mail* with the seals campaign. I was on the news desk at the *Times* and I remember when the story first surfaced and it was painted as a not very important story at all. David English, who was editor of the *Mail,* decided one day to do a splash on it. About three or four days later everybody else followed. And that is undoubtedly one of the turning points . . . and that was a case of the media actually leading the agenda.
>
> (anonymous interview, 28 July 1993; Anderson 1997: 143)

Anderson clearly shows that the campaign by the *Daily Mail* took hold and generated 150 newspaper articles across the British press in August 1988, a total of over 3000 column inches of coverage. However, the campaign led by the *Daily Mail* faded away without a clear verdict about what had caused the death of the seals, and we are left to ask what did it achieve. Anderson gives us two answers to consider. Peter Usher, a *Daily Mail* journalist, argued that the campaign aimed at heightening a general risk consciousness:

> . . . it didn't matter that the reason they were dying was a virus and that pollution couldn't be pinned down as the cause of the virus. It didn't matter because it just woke the realization that if you go on dumping chemicals in the seas you'll kill all the creatures in the sea. If you go on dumping chemicals in the land you'll kill all the creatures on the land. It's a very simple kind of realization but I think, I believe, that it was the seals that really drove the point home.
>
> (interview, 25 July 1989; Anderson 1997: 167)

Allan Mazur's (1998b) view is that sheer amount of coverage is very important and that the detail of coverage matters less in terms of grabbing and holding attention than the production of simple images – a dead seal pup or the idea of a hole in the ozone, for example. Anderson herself argues that environmentalists may lose credibility if no proven links between, for example, pollution and the viral infection are found and that, furthermore, this will push environmental action to mitigate risks and damage down the political agenda. What she did not suggest, but what now looks quite possible, is that the media reportage of the North Sea seals may well have had virtually no effect at all. In April 2000, many thousands of seals were reported dead in the Caspian Sea. *World Bank Development News* reported on 15 September as follows:

> Numerous possible contributors to seal mortality have been investigated in the past, including pollution from land-based sources, climatic effects such as absence of ice in the North Caspian Sea, parasitic worms, and other disease vectors. In 1997, a single Caspian seal was determined to have canine distemper virus infection, but seal disease could not be attributed directly to this virus at that time. The present study was designed to examine recent massive mortality in Caspian seals with these various causes in mind.

Seamus Kennedy and his colleagues then reported on the Caspian Sea outbreak in the following terms:

The epidemiology of canine distemper virus infection, including its effects on the Caspian Sea seal population . . . remains to be investigated . . . High levels of chemical contaminants have been recently identified in tissues of Caspian seals. As some of these substances have been shown to have immunotoxic effects in seals at the reported concentrations, further work is under way to determine whether pollutants contributed to their deaths.

(Kennedy *et al.* 2000: 639)

It is clear that the scientists know now where to look. To that extent there is progress. But the *Daily Mail*-led coverage may well not have contributed one iota to that advance, since the scientific and professional debate was well in advance of the journalism back in 1988, and the journalists are not concerned in 2000 to build on their previous efforts from twelve years before. We are then led to the social effects of such stories. Either a temporary distraction, perhaps with some immediate political pronouncement, as in the case of the Thatcher speech; or a contribution to an overall trend, where even a large campaign such as the one on North Sea seals will ultimately be seen as part of a cultural shift, whose reality and effects can only be hypothesized about. If we ask the question, 'How much science does the media give us?', is it too stark to reply that we get as much (and no more) as is necessary to sustain the appetite for information engendered by 'righteous indignation'? This would suggest, if there is a modicum of truth here, that our demand for information may often have less to do with being rational about risk than we might think. But perhaps we need to look at a different example.

Simon Watney (1988) argued that, throughout the 1980s, a significant portion of the media presented AIDS in such a way as to reproduce and even initiate stereotypes and condemnation. He noted that the image of society that formed the backcloth to much reporting on AIDS was often represented in terms of a brutal contrast between, on the one hand, the middle-American/Home Counties ideal of happy heterosexual couple with two children doing well at school and, on the other hand, a whole panorama of abject and pathetic examples of dysfunctionality: drug addicts, haemophiliacs[9] and homosexuals. For Watney this was a veritable bio-politics, and he saw that it actively prevented the transmission of knowledge by stigmatizing those organs prepared to offer rational advice to the communities most at risk. In the reportage of a field of risk for which science had most to say and most to offer, there were examples of dubious and obstructive spectacularization. Kimberly Bergalis was one such case.

She was the first person believed to have contracted AIDS through the professional activities of a health-worker. He was her dentist, David Acer, who continued to practise medicine – quite lawfully – while HIV-positive; he eventually died in 1990. Bergalis, who at that time had had the disease for over a year, went to the press after the Centers for Disease Control informed her of the likely source of her illness. She and her family received an insurance company compensation award partly based on the discovery of the same strains of HIV in her blood as were found in Dr. Acer's. Her case led to a national debate about whether health-care workers should be tested for HIV. She claimed that she rarely dated, had never had sex and did not use drugs. At the time she died in 1991 she was 23 years old. She probably contracted HIV in 1988 or 1989, at the age of 20 or 21. Senator Dannemeyer, a nationally known Republican politician from California, who had at least once represented President Bush on health issues and had, during the 1990s, campaigned for school prayer and against both the environmental lobby and advocates of liberal immigration, described his meeting with Bergalis as follows:

> . . . tears came to my eyes. My throat closed because I was in the presence of a saint. This young lady from Florida who is close to death with AIDS is a young saint. I felt like I was in the presence of Mother Teresa, and anybody who has met that lady knows they are in the presence of somebody very spiritual, or a word we do not use too much these days, very holy. She is a very holy person.
>
> (cited in Harrington 1997: 213)

The wide-spreading image of the AIDS victim as dead at the hands of the enemy (Park 1993) created a space for the characterization of that enemy, which was taken up in several ways. The struggle between scientists and retro-viruses certainly got some attention. But even if there could be agreement that defeating the virus was front-line, its transport channels, generally presented in terms of homosexuality, intravenous drug use and promiscuity, gained great prominence. Against this background, the Bergalis story set the tone for a substantial amount of public debate and when, quite close to death, she wrote to the Florida Health Authority (effectively to the nation), America took a great deal of notice:

I have lived to see my hair fall out, my body lose over 40 pounds, blisters on my sides. I've lived to go through nausea and vomiting, continual night sweats, chronic fevers of 103–104 that don't go away anymore . . . I lived through the fear of whether or not my liver has been completely destroyed by DDI and other drugs . . . I lived to see white fungus grow all over the inside of my mouth, the back of my throat, my gums and now my lips. It looks like white fur and it gives you atrocious breath. Isn't that nice? . . . I never used IV drugs, never slept with anyone and never had a blood transfusion. I blame Dr. Acer and every single one of you bastards. Anyone that knew Dr. Acer was infected and had full-blown AIDS and stood by not doing a damn thing about it. You are all just as guilty as he was. You've ruined my life.

(cited in Harrington 1997: 206–7)

The scene was set for politicians to demand compulsory HIV testing for health workers. One result[10] was that campaigning politicians and vocal victims began – through the media's feeding of the appetite for righteous indignation – to take on the role of 'risk-workers', partially eclipsing the risk-mitigation work done by health-workers, even at times transforming the image of health-workers from risk-workers to risk-producers, and competing with the scientific lobby for attention, power over resources and the right-to-determine-research agenda.

It is tempting to critique the media's role in obstructing the mitigation of risk. The reproduction of an audience over time requires a permanent renewal of their cultural consent to what is presented to them, and this may conflict with the rational action required to deal with emergent risk. The broad media agenda may appear tawdry when placed in the context of something like HIV – approximately 6.5 million deaths and 22 million HIV sufferers worldwide by 1997, according to the Centers for Disease Control, and by June 2000 suggestions of 23 million HIV sufferers in sub-Saharan Africa alone (Boseley 2000). It is, however, quite possible that there is a powerful structural logic at work, making – within the social system that we currently have – emotional spectacular-ization a necessary precondition to risk work on all fronts. The celebrity syndrome built around Kimberly Bergalis, or adapted in the case of such figures as Arthur Ashe or Rudolf Nureyev, may have been an important foundation for the behavioural change marked by the – many would say still insufficient and, as we will see, reversible – spread of protected sex and needle-exchange systems. The immediate consequences of public scapegoating, of gay men for example, have been and remain appalling. But the campaign for gay rights was not derailed by HIV and may even have been energized by it. Now this is not meant to be a defence of the media or a licence for heedless reportage. It remains the case that media treatment of complex issues is, with many honourable exceptions, generally lacking; a relevant example here being the 1994 *60 Minutes* broadcast, which cast doubt on Kimberly Bergalis's sexual inexperience but presented no adequate discussion of the DNA profiling that linked her strain of HIV to that of Dr. Acer's (Brown 1996).

According to Niklas Luhmann (2000: 12–13), topics such as seal deaths or AIDS are not originated in the media. They are drawn to our attention. How this happens is not explained by the medical science involved or by the interests of the doctors or their patients or the public at large. What matters is the success of the news item in getting our attention, in making sure that we watch and listen, in creating the possibility of follow-up items. From this point of view, which is to say from the point of view of the media, it may even be preferable if there is built-in controversy and plenty of room for disagreement. Was the dentist right or wrong to carry on working while HIV-positive? Was Kimberly Bergalis really so innocent? Is the seal story a cynical play on the soppy liberal love for dumb creatures, or are we really poisoning ourselves? For the media as a system, it will be optimal if positive and negative responses to their stories enter into equal battle: a conflict of views that flares brightly for a while – sustaining high energy levels for the producers and a keen interest among the consumers – and is then replaced by the next *cause célèbre*. This is quite a distance from the mode of communication required for a rational discourse on risks.

Cultural Variation or Cultural Rupture?

We have seen that although the precise measurement of risk is sometimes possible, it is not the paradigm case. Estimation of risk is generally what is needed, but standards of acceptability may vary across cultures. We have noted that some risks are ignored as extrinsic: the company board cannot consider how to remove the risks to their competitors should a new product be successful. On top of this we have learned that much of what we know about risks comes to us through an interwoven media complex driven by the need for audience retention in the age of the visual image. And we may have been disappointed that the risks that the media do amplify are not necessarily reduced as a result of that temporary increase in volume. This leads us to a complex but compelling question: Are we, then, dealing only with multiple risk contexts, each with different characteristics (knowledge, standards, procedures, expectations), as if there were clear lines in the social world between, for example, pesticide manufacture in India, sexual behaviour in San Francisco and waste dumping in the North Sea? Or are we, at least in the industrial/post-industrial world, dealing with one dominant risk culture and, if we are, has it changed (from one determined by the mercantile worldview to one under the sign of the visual image, for example)? Whether cultures are split or not, and whether they are changed or not, we are dealing with the issue of culture(s). How do we think about culture(s)?

Mary Douglas has become one of the world's leading anthropologists over the last fifty years.[1] Looking back over her career in 1999, she hinted that the problem of understanding risk 'is how to take a grip on a whole world'. She then spoke of a change that occurred between 1966 and 1970:

When in 1966 I chose the title *Purity and Danger* with a subtitle refer-
ring to theories of pollution I did not imagine that both purity and
danger would be linked in a world-wide anxiety about pollution of
water and air, and the environment. But by 1970, the topic of
'Environments at risk' had become prominent, and has been ever
since.

(Douglas 1999: ix)

She is also on record from 1997 saying that risk analysis is 'a
whole new field', emerging from a coincidence of industrialists,
politicians and journalists (Douglas 1999: 224). Relying on Douglas
as our introduction to the question of risk and culture, we get a clear
response to the question of risk culture or risk cultures. She will tell
us that there are multiple risk cultures, each of them capable of
being analysed using the same basic categories of social form. In
Douglas's worldview, risk is ephemeral. Despite her preparedness
to allow for the emergence of new social categories, she expects
them not to upset the social order and requires that they fit into the
world that she has in her grip. In her view, different cultures are to
be expected, but the types of group behaviour to be encountered
there will be the same. This is not surprising. She came out of the
British anthropological tradition of comparative cultural analysis,
rejected evolutionism after giving it virtually no consideration in
Purity and Danger, and opted for a quite austere formalism. As her
biographer Richard Fardon (1999: 260) put it, 'enormous diversity
is distilled into relatively simple criteria of form'.[2] These formal
criteria of social behaviour provide the same fixed possibilities of
social action whether one is dealing with a society ruled by witchcraft or one obsessed with risk. As we will see, what this does is to
give rigour to Mary Douglas's thought on risk. It also, however,
rules out the possibility that there may have been a fundamental
cultural rupture creating a risk-sensitive society in which the formal
options for group behaviour are changed. There is, however, a tradition of cultural analysis that is based upon the idea of such
epistemological breaks; we will look at this after considering the
work of Mary Douglas in more detail.

The formal sociology of risk

When Mary Douglas presented her 1970 lecture, 'Environments at
risk', her thoughts were still taking shape. She observed that most
societies host beliefs in some sort of God and also fears for their

environment. She thought that emerging ecological concerns would be motivated by abhorrence at defilement of the sacred. However, the idea of the sacred did not retain its place among the foundational concepts of her social thinking for very long. What did eventually remain was a belief that the the cultural conditioning of definitions of environmental risk was overlaid on a fixed social ontology. This began to be secured by her own research work in the Belgian Congo:

> The Lele regarded the short dry season as unbearably hot. They had their sayings and rules about how to endure its heat. 'Never strike a woman in the dry season', for example, 'or she will crumple up and die because of the heat'. They longed for the first rains as relief from the heat. On the other bank of the Kasai, the Bushong agreed with the Belgians that the dry season was pleasantly cool and they dreaded the onset of the first rains [and the hot season]. Fortunately the Belgians had made excellent meteorological records, and I found that in terms of solar radiation, diurnal and nocturnal temperatures, cloud cover, etc., there was very little objective difference that could entitle one season to be called strictly hotter than the other.
>
> (Douglas 1999: 207)

As she goes on to show, the explanation for the differing definitions, by the Lele, Bushong and Belgians, of the 'same' set of conditions is rooted in the different social regimes of the three groups, with the Lele and Bushong farming their land differently, while the Belgians followed bureaucratic usage in the capital, even though the temperature differentials there did not obtain on the banks of the Kasai.

For Douglas, views of the environment inevitably arise out of the systems of social ordering and are part of the socio-institutional clothing that covers this frame. The Lele believed that their population was under attack by sorcerors; forty years later, many Californians think that passive smoking is one of the greatest risks to their health. For Douglas, these phenomena can be subjected to the same form of sociological analysis: social institutions, cultural beliefs, self-understanding and apparently objective characterization of the physical world, each fits in different but related ways into an overall world picture, which is different in the case of the Lele in 1960 and twenty-first century Californians, but which cloaks the same social ontology. As Douglas (1999) puts it, 'The view of the universe and a particular kind of society holding this view are closely interdependent. They are a single system' (p. 212). Risk preoccupations, for Douglas, act as one of the elements of social superstructure. They rest on what she thinks of as universal principles of human motivation and necessity formation. As she puts it, 'Telling each other that there is no time, that we can't afford it, that God wouldn't like it, and that it is against nature and our children will suffer, these are the means by which we adapt our society to our environment, and it to ourselves' (p. 213). And Douglas goes on to note that it is tiring to have to make the same arguments all the time, that things need to settle down into systems that we can take for granted. The money economy did that, the nuclear family did that. The question posed by the closing paragraphs of her 1970 lecture is whether the emergence of a new form of risk discourse in the last third of the twentieth century constitutes a step towards such another such system.[3] She waited a decade before giving the implicit answer that it did not. But her answer did not privilege risk in any particular way. It was just that she was temperamentally disinclined against most of the potential components of any such system (all those linking to rationality, for example).

The starting point of *Risk and Culture: An Essay in the Selection of Technological and Environmental Dangers*, published in 1982 and co-written with political scientist Aaron Wildavsky, was that since the 1960s, 'confidence about the physical world has turned into doubt. Once the source of safety, science and technology have become the source of risk'. The authors ask, 'What could have happened in so short a time to bring forward so severe a reaction? How can we explain the sudden widespread, across-the-board concern about environmental pollution and personal contamination that has arisen in the Western world?' (Douglas and Wildavsky 1982: 10). They answer that the material world of business, technology, money and markets has come to be seen as polluted, and that there is a widespread view that we ought to be able to afford a cleaner physical and social environment. So, the culture that created material wealth has created a distrust of it and an opposition to such developments as the growth of airports (Milch 1976), the building of nuclear power plants (Nelkin and Pollak 1981) and the needless expense and pollution of the space programme (Rodrigue 2001).

To complicate matters, Douglas now has to contend with ideological opponents. When, in 1970, she was inside the anthropological fold, she paid alternative views little attention. Now, in 1982, she has to combat those thinkers who believe that risk issues can be resolved rationally. So, Douglas and Wildavsky make a set of socio-cultural arguments. In the first place, they explain that risk behaviour is not rational. Consider, they suggest, that the cost of each life 'saved' by the seat-belt laws is estimated at $3600, yet the drawing up and imposition of vinyl chloride standards probably cost $7.5m for each life saved. What rationality could make sense of that disparity? If it cost a quarter of a million dollars for scientists to spend the two years needed to test a single chemical on 300 mice to see if it is carcinomic, according to what rationality are we going to deal with the 45,000 commercially utilized chemicals, let alone the other 4.5 million chemical compounds for which we have found no use yet (Douglas and Wildavsky 1982: 53)? They add that we cannot begin to list all of the risks to which we are subject, because estimates of risk vary from one social group to another, and there is no single reference point, even within the scientific community, from which to make a risk register.[4] There is, they conclude, no definitive list of the risks to which we are subject. There is no set of rationally defensible risk priorities. The classifications of risk that we follow, they tell us, arise out of our culture and can vary from one culture to another. Which risks, at what level, are acceptable to which groups of people is always a social question.[5]

Now, some twenty years later, we can see more clearly that both the aggressive commercial exploitation of techno-scientific research and the protests that the hyper-utilization of human and natural resources has gone much too far share the same language, the language of risk – the feeling that future horrible events of great magnitude are just around the corner unless we do something now. Yet on each side different conclusions are drawn: if we don't keep innovating, we will not be able to look after our old people; if we do not reduce our energy consumption, sea levels will rise. The discourse of risk is dialogic and dynamic. Its basic structure of syntax and semantics is not solely scientific, mathematical, logical or objective, even though each of these plays hugely important parts. It is cultural, social, political. Each scientific finding or logical conclusion may be true as a single statement. When, however, one or more of them is associated with other, similarly 'true' assertions, and thereby combined into a broadcast narrative, which, serving some interests and not others, emphasizes some 'risks' while erasing others – and this is the normal process of risk communication – then we are undeniably dealing with the cultural and political.

Table 3.1   Risk in terms of knowledge and consent (with examples)

Knowledge[6] AND consent	Consent WITHOUT full knowledge
An agreed priority: any problems are technical and they can be solved through calculation or trial and error *Example*: monitoring of national economic performance to warn of inflation/recession risk	It is agreed the problems need resolving, but we need to improve the state of knowledge *Example*: the treatment of AIDS
Knowledge WITHOUT consent	**NEITHER consent NOR full knowledge**
The problems are recognized and we know how to reduce them significantly, but there is no agreement that we should act comprehensively *Example*: smoking-induced lung cancer	We do not know enough, and cannot agree to priority-setting on the basis of one approach *Example*: rehabilitation of sex offenders

Source: Adapted from Douglas and Wildavsky (1982: 5).

Where, then, should the analysis of risk in society begin? Douglas and Wildavsky argued that the key concepts are knowledge and consent, and their analysis is that there are four possibilities which arise from the possible associations of positive or negative states of knowledge and of consent. Table 3.1 is adapted from their work.

If risk is seen as a function of degrees of knowledge about the future and degrees of consent about desired outcomes, then we can see that there would be no such thing as non-social risk. Douglas illustrates this with another example from the Lele, who, in the middle of tropical diseases, leprosy, malaria and wild animals, most fear being struck by lightning. This is not a rational prioritizing of risk fears, and Douglas argues that this lack of apparent rationality is a normal attribute of beliefs about risk. She further exemplifies this by comparing the fear of asbestos-induced lung cancer with the fear of sun-induced skin cancer, and wonders why so many still sunbathe and why so few face exposure to asbestos with equanimity. Overall, it is her view that each society or sub-culture elevates some risks – and, it must be added, some benefits – to a high point while depressing others out of sight. In other words, although there are surely ways of minimizing specific risks, there are no sure ways of reducing the level of risk in general. Such a policy horizon would be chimerical.

Although the field of science and technology has, for Douglas, seen a change in the late twentieth century, with the move towards a shared public discourse of risk, this does not necessarily indicate, as we have already hinted, a complete lack of comparability between contemporary western culture and other social forms. Douglas and Wildavsky (1982) see one particular similarity between the risk condition of advanced and earlier societies. Asking the question, 'Why is there such eco-concern now?', they point out that technological knowledge has enlarged the scope for making someone pay for each misfortune we undergo (p. 33). But while we may say that the demystification of the modern world through the growth of science has increased the rational attributability of blame for events, Douglas also notes that pre-technological societies were also regimes of blame, with 'magical' explanations for every harm. Evans-Pritchard (1937), writing in the 1930s on witchcraft among the Azande, thought that magical explanations were comparable to a westerner's recourse to notions of bad luck or good fortune. So, just like noting that someone's success was due to being in the right place at the right time is quite compatible with a belief in science, so it is that the demise of magical worldviews in the West does not mean goodbye to the practices of blaming and scapegoating that used to accompany them. Even though these practices of blaming and exculpation are now ensnared in complex legal, scientific and historical narratives, no one, Douglas tells us, should believe that contemporary practice is more rational than its earlier 'equivalent'.

While Douglas and Wildavsky do concentrate their focus at the level of group and societal cultures, they are aware of the importance of the actions of individual agents, even if their frame of reference does not stretch to embrace the interactional negotiation of specific situations by these agents. Their use of individual examples tends to be illustrative of cultural structures, rather than descriptive of actual situations. For example, the existence of strategic disagreements between scientists underlines the argument that science and technology cannot be treated as a simple reference point with respect to the understanding of environmental risk.[7] Thus they tell us about Samuel Epstein, professor of occupational and environmental medicine at the University of Illinois Medical Center, who ran a campaign in the 1980s that claimed that cancer deaths were on the increase due substantially to environmental factors, helping to cause something approaching a moral panic in the United States. Then they explain that the evidence on which such claims and beliefs were founded was interpreted differently by authoritative figures, and was inherently capable of being manipulated:

> To find out what happens with low doses of carcinogens, 24,192 mice were subjected to seven different doses of a known carcinogen. So far, the results seem to show that there is a threshold for bladder but not for liver tumours. But ... the megamouse study has generated a certain amount of controversy. The basic difficulty is that the dose rates are so small and the observed incidences are close to error rates so that, for example, changing results in eleven out of 8000 animals in one set of data might reverse the findings.
>
> (Douglas and Wildavsky 1982: 54)

One of their other examples concerns a professor of radiological physics who alleged that declining scores in school IQ tests were due to nuclear fall-out from bomb tests, and that there was a rise in infant mortality due to the Three Mile Island incident. His allegations were responded to by Dr. Arthur Tamplin, of the National Resources Defense Council, who said, 'Dr. Sternglass never completes his studies. He doesn't go back several years to see what kinds of fluctuations might be expected, and he does not examine enough different areas to get meaningful data' (Douglas and Wildavsky 1982: 60). You do not have to be an expert on Max Weber's work concerning value-relevance to know that the decision to regard a piece of social investigation as complete is always somewhat arbitrary, and is made – reasonably or not – in the given context with reference to particular (even if not well understood) horizons of meaning and significance.

In showing us how scientists disagree about levels of risk, Douglas and Wildavsky were inevitably drawn to the issue of risk assessment in general. We saw earlier that risks can often be calculated with precision, or at least rigorously estimated on the basis of past experience. We know that the life assurance business has been going strong for a long time, based as it is on actuarial principles. Banking is a secure institution, yet it risks (in apparent safety, at least most of the time) lending more than it has on deposit, knowing that in normal circumstances all the deposit holders are not going to turn up on the same day and ask for their money. Research programmes in leading universities may try in the laboratory to duplicate the energy levels which obtain in the sun, and we hear of this in admiration rather than fear for our lives. So when Douglas and Wildavsky ask if 'professional' methods of risk assessment tell us what risks we face, it will come as no surprise to hear that their conclusion is that such risk assessment is biased. This may, however, seem a premature conclusion, given the methodologies pointed to in Chapter 1 and, in particular, all the techniques of the calculative paradigm that are available. Surely it would be an exaggeration to claim that there is no methodology that, in particular cases, can eliminate bias and render some predictability into the realm of risk assessment?

The way that Douglas and Wildavsky saw things, at the level now of individual options for risk assessment, there are three principal methods which are available. They refer to them as revealed preference, expressed preference and cost–benefit analysis. All three ask the question, 'What risks will you take?' The method of revealed preference is essentially sociological research based on observation (and we will see in the next chapter that we do not have enough of it). It is based on the observation of the actual risks that people do take. Drawing policy conclusions on the basis of revealed preference research may assume that what obtained in the past will continue to obtain. As a foundation for social policy or for actuarial-type calculation, it does tend to assume that existing social and economic arrangements are a kind of default standard. It does, however, have the profound advantage that it can be rigorous, and that what people have been doing is very often a good guide to what they will be doing. The second method for answering the question 'What risks will you take?' is that of finding out people's expressed preferences. In other words, you ask them. The technology of the survey, focus group, consultation exercise and psychometric test provides the means. Expressed and revealed preference methodologies are, of course, subject to the standard array of critiques and cautions that may be levelled at empirical social research methods (representativeness of the sample, acuity of the instrument, integrity of the respondents, limitations of the inferences). The third method is somewhat imperialist. If the first two try to ask what people do and what people want, this third method aspires to tell us what we ought to do, what is most rational. It is cost–benefit analysis. It assumes that economic measures are always appropriate, and that all goods can be rendered in economic terms and thereby compared. Douglas is particularly critical of cost–benefit analysis.[8] Her sense of actual risk behaviour – that we inherit risk preferences from our culture, that we screen out some possibilities from our consciousness routinely, that we select our focus, weigh alternatives through some kind of common cultural understanding, that we edit problems, and do things like smoke even though we are repeatedly told it will probably cause us harm – all of this means that the decontextualizing economic calculus of cost–benefit analysis impoverishes our understanding of risk behaviour and weakens any policy process that is overdependent on it.

In the extended macrosocial and political commentary that makes up the second half of *Risk and Culture*, Douglas and Wildavsky (1982) present a structural analysis that links the dominant modes of risk concern within the culture, at any given time, to the kind of reaction within the society or sub-societal enclave this is likely to mean. Their key categories here are hierarchies, markets, sectarian groups and individuals. In Douglas's work on risk, these are nothing less than her Kantian categories. And the secret heresy (for an anthropologist) of Douglas's approach is that this makes risk epiphenomenal, because culture itself is epiphenomenal, subordinate to the transcendental categories of subjectivity and social form – as we will now see:

> ... the hierarchist ... is focused on dangers of foreign relations ... risks of economic collapse are ever-present to the mind of the market individualist ... risks from technology are uppermost in the sectarian mind ... all three positions, individualism, hierarchy, and sectarianism are extremes. None is prima facie attractive. The ruthlessness of power-seeking in a free-market society has been exposed often enough. The clogged inertia and cruel caste distinctions of hierarchy similarly ... the sectarian way tends to present humans as victims to be compensated and weaklings to be protected.
>
> (Douglas and Wildavsky 1982: 188–90)

Table 3.2 gives one cross-section of Douglas and Wildavsky's view of the result of perceived growth towards crisis point in response to three particular forms of societal risk.

It is possible that the four categories – hierarchies, markets, sects and individualists – could be utterly indispensible to the description and analysis of risk contexts, but we have insufficient evidence to be confident. Douglas and Wildavsky closed[9] their discussion of science and technology with a sustained examination of environmental pressure groups. They asked what would happen if Greenpeace, Friends of the Earth and other such organizations succeed in dictating the political agenda:

The unintended results of a full flowering of sectarian politics would be a larger, weaker government and a smaller economy. The economy would shrink as resources are used to prevent dangers; the bureaucracy would grow as it regulates the risks people are allowed to take. There will be many more rules, true; but since the rulers will not be respected, their authority to regulate will also be undermined. Government will be bigger, but it will not be stronger; openness and participation will only lead to unanswerable criticism. For the society in general this will mean enhanced conflict over a smaller pie, without a cohesive centre to moderate the resulting disputes.

(Douglas and Wildavsky 1982: 183–4)

This picture is an ideal-type, a one-sided accentuation from a particular point of view, as Weber put it. In this case, it is a developed and admittedly overemphasized hypothesis, seen at the start of the 1980s, as to how we might develop following the 'green' agenda. In 1988, Mary Douglas (1992a: 267–8) said, in Zurich, that central governments believed that there was a serious threat to the biosphere. If that meant, and continues to mean, that the 'green' agenda has been partially accepted by the central hierarchies, the

Table 3.2   Examples of risk response from hierarchical, sectarian and individualist political systems

Risks of human violence (terrorism, crime waves, war)	Traditional diffuse hierarchical structures, with their vague multiple goals, avoidance of change and slow sequential problem-solving, come under threat: leading to censorship, compartmentalization and (ultimately) martial law
Risks from technology	Sectarian interests rise (e.g. green movement pressure groups): leading to disrespectful and weakening attacks on the centre, idealism of the eventual future but abiding pessimism now, increased intolerance of inequality, factional disputes, appeasement through regulation proliferation, more complex government, intrusive bureaucracy and weaker economy
Risks of economic failure	Individualism is reinforced, but systems for handling monopoly tendencies, various kinds of 'loophole' abuse, wealth redistribution, economic crime, management incompetence and poverty come under intense public scrutiny

political scientists can now ask to what extent the hypothesized consequences of such an acceptance have materialized (see, for example, Padgett 1989).[10] Circumstances have changed, however, since 1982. Questions have become differently framed, and we still do not have the evidence that might strengthen the case for her Kantian categories. Their general cultural relevance remains somewhat short of the synthetic *a priori* status to which they aspire. But let us see what happens when they are sought out as the precondition of the experience of AIDS.

Fault lines

Douglas is unable to focus on the single risk-taker. This is not a category that she recognizes. Her thought will not attend to a social unit smaller than the group, even though her categories are those of transcendental subjectivity. Her approach to the individual, self or person – whatever label one elects to use – is through the group and its culture. The possibilities of action for an individual emerge from the forms of the collective, but these are the generalized conditions of the four forms of the transcendental ego. As she put it in a lecture which she gave in 1990, 'self and community have to be examined together' (Douglas 1992a: 232). She understands that some risks are routine within some groups, whereas in others those same risks might not even be contemplated. Some groups exercise careful self-surveillance, whereas others do not. In discussing AIDS, she writes, 'A refusal to take sound hygienic advice is not to be attributed to weakness of understanding. It is a preference. To account for preferences, there is only cultural theory' (Douglas 1992b: 102), by which she means the understanding of the way that cultural superstructures are built onto the basic ontological form. Her methodology is macrosociological, dependent upon textual evidence (especially noticeable in the work with Wildavsky) or reported action, and theory-driven, rather than classically anthropological – that is to say, based on observation of primary interactions. It would not be easy to make rich ethnography clothe her formal frame.

Risk and Culture tells us that contemporary societies can be seen to consist of four different structural types: hierarchies, markets, sectarian clusters and individuals.[11] This four-fold classification is repeated in adapted form to understand the predetermined possibilities for individuals relating to risk. For any given situation,

individuals will be, more or less, members of the central community, the entrepreneurial frontier, a dissident enclave or they will
be isolates. The central community, at the core of city life for
example, has a strong definition of deviance, backs it up with a clear
view of what natural dangers there are, and is alert to provide
surveillance against them. This structure of surveillance is hierarchical, ordered, consensual. In speaking of AIDS, she says, 'When
the epidemic comes we would expect this part of the city to tighten
its defences, to become more punishing and more controlling'
(Douglas 1992b: 104). The perspective here is borne out by the UK
reaction to the foot and mouth crisis in 2001.

Urban society always has recalcitrant and rebellious minorities,
which Douglas calls dissenting enclaves. The centre rejects their
values and makes them into an enclave; and because the centre is
ordered and hierarchical, the enclave rejects these principles. The
enclave is, for Douglas, an important ingredient in understanding
AIDS as risk. The third archetype is the individualist, who does not
commit either to the core or to the enclave, but who can be useful
and a temporary member of either or both. The stereotype is the
entrepreneur, the frontier scout of market society. The last type is
the isolate: ineffectual, fatalist, victim; rarely isolated by choice, the
isolate is the past object of predation.

Modern risk culture is, then, in Douglas's thinking, quadrilateral
in form, and the main lines of power and response run across the
diagonal between individualist and central community. The line
from enclave to isolate is in tension with this diagonal of power.
The central community is the place of dominant knowledge, the
locus of the professions and of expertise. The enclave rejects some
parts or even all of this: 'the enclave counsels against adulterated
foods, against stimulants and sedatives, and artificial additives. Its
stylistic preference is for homespun, folkloristic remedies. It is
inevitably against the industrial mass production of fast foods'
(Douglas 1992b: 109). In the field of knowledge, the individualists
are cosmopolitan, trend-setters in taste and fashion, unorthodox
and risk-taking in their personal habits: they will die of high blood
pressure, heart disease, lung cancer. For Douglas, even when they
fall ill, this means one more stage on which to show their flair and
modern spirit. In older language, they are the vanguard of the petit-
bourgeoisie (Boyne 2000a: 8–9). In complete contradistinction, the
isolates are eccentric, as likely to blame God or conspiring neighbours for their misfortunes.

At each of the four corners of the risk quadrilateral, the culture of risk will be different. In the case of AIDS, the liberal individualists want tolerance while the central community advise rectitude and hygiene. The social worker, working within the enclave and encouraging self-reliance, leans away from central definitions of the situation. Meanwhile, the formless mass of isolates are the source of the miasma that fuels drug-paranoia and campaigns of immigrant expulsion. The central community wants to erect a *cordon sanitaire*, a second skin around the body. Home had always been a safe place, the infection was brought back here from elsewhere. The notion that infections first come from outside leads to caution and surveillance and, as long as the danger can be kept outside, the attention paid to it can be marginal. The central community is, as Douglas says (1992b: 117), risk-averse, and its risk-aversion is part of its border control. Within the gay enclave, there is partial rejection of the central community, but still some repetition of the notion of double protection: both skin and the enclave community. Medical definitions have been accepted, a level of risk also taken. Douglas concludes that the further the socio-economic-cognitive gap between the central community and the periphery, the more punitive will be the reactions from the centre.

The anthropological fieldwork done in Britanny by Mary Douglas and her colleagues led to the publication of an article entitled 'The self as risk-taker' (Douglas 1992b), but in truth the self as a concept or reality hardly existed there. The key relationship was between the beliefs developing within the central hierarchy and the different ones within the dissenting enclave. Even the universal phenomenon of blaming[12] rapidly goes through the level of the individual to that of the group. As Kimberly Bergalis said, 'Anyone that knew Dr. Acer was infected and had full-blown AIDS and stood by not doing a damn thing about it. You are all just as guilty as he was' (cited in Harrington 1997: 207). In Douglas's cultural sociology, the fault lines and the risk lines overlap. They run between social groups, and from group to event (whether imagined or not) and from event to group. The self, whether as the source of rational choice or as accidental single victim, exists as a mark of exemplification. It is perhaps here that one crucial weakness of the cultural group approach to risk arises, since the attenuation of the role of the individual does tend to divorce the discourse of risk from that of responsibility. After Kant constructed his transcendental categories, he found it necessary to formulate a moral law as a precondition for society. Despite Douglas's Kantianism, she has not moved clearly in that direction, although it may be that her commitment to the category of blame is some sort of equivalent.

There is little doubt that Douglas's work constitutes an influential body of work concerning risk and culture, and also that it can be used to understand change within cultures, but some of its utility is dependent upon its basic model being correct. In this respect, it is problematic that Douglas's view that human groups have a small range that is set *a priori*, and that the possible variety of individual behaviour follows from that, has not been more rigorously tested through ethnography and through psychometric method. Her four modes of group and individual form could have been subjected to empirical test, even though from a Kantian view such an exercise on transcendental categories could be superfluous. It is quite hard to know, aside from all of this, why her approach to risk has not founded a truly vigorous research programme, unless it is that the glitter of variety, a myriad of cultures overlaid on the same social forms, mattered more. When Lewis Coser wrote about her using Isaiah Berlin's image of the fox, who knows many things, and the hedgehog, who knows one big thing, he concluded that 'Mary Douglas is very much a fox' (cited in Fardon 1999: 243), and this may help to explain why her work on risk does not rest on more substantial empirical foundations.

The emerging rival within the field of the cultural analysis of risk may be Robert Castel. His work on risk is less developed, but does rest on alternative theoretical foundations and also has significant empirical referents. He believes that the classic individual (which has four varieties in Douglas's work) was a part of an earlier world, that the very production of the individual has changed. No longer simply emergent from hierarchies or sects or bouncing between the two with positive or negative spin, for Castel individuals are coming to be seen as combinations of factors of risk.

Social transformation

Robert Castel, co-founder with Michel Foucault and Pierre Bourdieu of the Vincennes sociology department in 1979, and one of that brilliant generation of French social scientists (Bourdieu, Foucault, Boltanski, Touraine, Moscovici) that emerged in the 1960s, researches macrosocial transformations. He has carried out this work in two areas: the institutions of mental health and the deconstruction of wage labour. His work is historically informed, and he focuses on cultural changes over time. Although he is not as vigorous an advocate of the absolute epistemological breaks that one finds described in the work of Gaston Bachelard, Louis Althusser or the Michel Foucault of *The Order of Things,* his work does suggest that, at least in these hugely important areas of social risk – mental health and employment – the great changes that have taken place over the last thirty years amount to a social metamorphosis.[13]

His 1982 book *The Management of Risks* comments upon the changes that had taken place in France within the field of mental illness. Since the 1960s, the professional definition of this field, formerly dominated by psychiatric medicine and, to a lesser extent, psychoanalysis, has been opened up to engagement with many other disciplines: social scientific, historical, artistic (Castel 1982: 19). The general view may be that this links to the critique of repression that climaxed with the student movements of 1968. The French psychiatric profession, however, saw these cultural upheavals as providing the opportunity for thoroughgoing reform, and the reforms led to increasing administrative control. The replacement of an asylum model with a community psychiatry one was to be enabled by the 'establishment of a specialised body of professionals and specific institutions', a 'complete synthesis, bringing together technical, theoretical, institutional, and legislative dimensions . . . the exercise of mental medicine becoming at the limit co-extensive with the social ensemble as a whole' (p. 42). The question of prevention or cure now arises – 'better to prevent than manage' is a catchphrase which Castel uses later (p. 131) – and the scene is set for wholesale change in the management of risk in this area. The reduction of the population of mental patients in hospitals took some time. Indeed, it probably grew during the 1970s (pp. 61–2), despite the talk of de-institutionalization. As Castel points out, resources were an issue, much of what was available being spent on large increases in the numbers of trained professionals, and there were numerous points of inertia and resistance. Nevertheless, Castel argues, the development and expansion of public psychiatry in France sets the model for the medical territorialization of the society through the means of a technical administration operating with sophisticated classificatory schemes (p. 73).

Against this background, the understanding of the therapeutic process is rapidly transformed. Henri Laborit is quoted from 1977 speaking of bio-neuro-psycho-sociological integration (Castel 1982: 113), and Castel wonders whether we are beginning to see the individual as the sum of the points of view contributed by the various branches of positive knowledge. Is this a new positivism? Whatever the answer to this question, the systemic developments he describes mean a weakening of the psychiatrist's power to make judgements of risk, since although remaining crucial the psychiatrist becomes now only one of the forces in play.

For Castel, the humanistic focus on the individual, the diagnosis of whether he or she is essentially dangerous or not, is no longer prime. Its methodological significance has been drastically reduced with the change of focus from the individual to levels of risk within a population.[14] Each mental patient was previously thought to carry a threat, but who could be sure whether this potential would be realized? Operating at the level of the individual, it can easily be thought that what is harmless today may be dangerous tomorrow. Faced with such conundrums, it would be quite rational for a psychiatrist to opt for prudence and preventive intervention. If there was any doubt over a case, it was better to take steps to neutralize the potential threat. No one could ever show that such a decision had been wrong. Whereas if a lunatic was allowed loose and harm ensued, then the error of judgement would be there for all to see. To place the single case at the centre of this safety-first problematic has considerable economic and social costs. How, we now ask in puzzlement, could the ideal of confining all those who were suspected of being potentially a danger to themselves or others have functioned as the policy horizon, as the goal to aim at in the mental health field? Could that take care of all the danger? Would it really be possible to hospitalize all who were suspected of being dangerous? Treating dangerousness as a latent and irreducible quality of individuals led down a road without end. In part, the reformation of the psychiatric profession examined by Castel allowed this earlier individual-centred methodology to be superseded.

There had been signposts to an alternative mode of analysis. In the mid-nineteenth century, Morel had proposed a view based on 'assessment of the frequency of mental illnesses and other abnormalities among the most disadvantaged strata of the population' (Castel 1982: 148). He was talking the demographic, distributional language of risk, and was interested in the correlations between various indicators, like poor housing, malnutrition, alcohol usage and sexual behaviour. His thought anticipated later statistical studies of populations, such as that on suicide by Emile Durkheim, but he had no techniques for treatment and adminis- tration other than the case-by-case methodology. There had also been the eugenics movement. Eugenic reasoning operates in terms of risk at the level of populations, rather than potential danger at the level of the individual unit. But the eugenic path did not widen, in large part because of the discreditable development of both theory and practice in National Socialist Germany.[15] For Castel, just as the individual case comes to be seen to be not about a particular unique individual, but rather an assemblage of judge- ments across an epistemological spectrum, so a population can be actuarially analysed to reveal its likely percentage of members at risk, and that population can be tested to indicate those at risk. As Castel puts it:

> A risk does not arise from the presence of particular, precise danger embodied in a particular concrete individual or group. It is the effect of a combination of abstract *factors* which render more or less prob- able the occurrence of undesirable modes of behaviour.
>
> (Castel 1982: 287)

Castel's example is the French infant management system known as GAMIN (*Gestion automatisées de médecine infantile*). Following a law passed in 1970, three compulsory post-natal examinations were introduced: in the first few days, after a few months and at two years. The tests look at mother and child over a range of physical, psychological and social attributes. The individual responses are not the triggers for alarm and action, it is their combination that may set off an early warning. Here risk identification stems from multi-factorial coincidence. It does not arise here from minor occurrence and the subsequent danger of aggravated repetition, in the way that the world is often presented in hospital soap operas, which still see the world in individualist terms. To organize the reaction to the early signs given by the examinations, a new part of the French health system began to emerge in 1976. This was the CAMSP (*Centre d'Action Médico-Sociale Précoce*), the aim of which was to identify anomalies, diagnose the underlying con- ditions and establish a treatment and support regime. Over the years since their introduction, they have focused increasingly on the handicapped pre-school child, bringing their expertise to the family in time of need. Some centres specialize in one particular area of handicap, whereas others are more general. All, however, are especially concerned to try to see the total picture, to enable them in particular to register and respond to the conditions that are not so easily seen. The technological base is bureaucratic and epidemiological. When action is triggered by the readings on the 'instrumentation', it is presented as supportive and child-centred.

Castel does think the advanced urban-bureaucratic world did change following 1968, and in such a way that the emergent risk-discourse and its objects of analysis were thoroughly changed from a scientific model of knowledge faced with an individual case, into combinations of perspectives leading to multi-factorial judgements.[16] This was not an absolute break, but – to borrow a formulation from his later work (Castel 1995: 16) – means understanding that events and developments in the past allowed the present to become different. It is something of a riddle that Mary Douglas, the anthropologist of culture, emerging from the tradition of rigorous fieldwork, should find that, beneath the appearances of difference, the structure of social life remains unaltered. Yet, Robert Castel, the structural sociologist, insists that superficial similarities may need to be read differently since underlying structures have changed. We will not, in this book, be able to solve that riddle, which may in any event be a basic gestalt of the human sciences, but we will return to the question of cultural rupture when we consider the work of Ulrich Beck in the final chapter. For the time being, we need to note the importance of the basic distinction between the two approaches examined in this chapter. Mary Douglas asserts the ephemerality of risk and the permanent presence of transcendental forms of being, while Castel's approach (and perhaps those of others yet to come) allows the possibility of thoroughgoing reconstruction, in which context risk may be currently at the very foundation of it.

Risk-taking

What happens when risks are taken consciously? Mary Douglas does not usually give us case studies, nor does Robert Castel. Statisticians working for underwriting firms in the insurance industry do not as a rule drill down to individual cases. This does not mean there is no interest in describing or modelling individual risk behaviour – quite the contrary. The structure of individual decision-making under uncertainty is modelled by economists, philosophers, mathematicians and cognitive psychologists. The stresses and routines of individual risk-takers, whether in Formula One racing cars or on the side of a sheer cliff, are also brought to the fascinated attention of the masses by features journalism. We can start to examine the question of the single risk-taker with an everyday example.

Amniocentesis is one of the most common invasive pre-natal diagnostic procedures. It is undertaken as a screening procedure for Down's syndrome and for spina bifida. The procedure involves the insertion of a needle through the mother's abdomen and into the amniotic sac to draw a sample of amniotic fluid. A 1986 study by Tabor *et al.* provides part of the basis for advice still given to mothers contemplating having the procedure (Whittle 2000). The study concluded that risk of miscarriage, following the procedure, is increased by 1 per cent. Mary Douglas provides a personal example:

> A member of my family recently went for a test to the maternity clinic and discovered that she had a one in two hundred probability of bearing a Down's Syndrome baby. The news was given on the telephone. She was offered a further test, but warned that the amniocentesis held a one in a hundred probability of damaging the foetus . . . When she

burst into tears, they told her to make up her mind quickly whether she wanted the test or not, because it was nearly five o'clock, and they had to go home.

(Douglas 1992a: 14)

Douglas commented that this scenario was another sign of cultural change, and she explained her remark by saying that previously the local doctor would have told her that it was probably best to have the procedure. We can make the contrast a little more precise by comparing the situation which she described to the one profiled by Elaine May and Otto Preminger in the 1971 film *Such Good Friends*. Here there is also a concern for statistics. When the husband is admitted to hospital, the first complication is occasioned by an adverse reaction, and the family are told afterwards that it only occurs in one case in ten thousand. The second complication which kills him is even rarer. The grieving wife is told that this was one case in 50,000. The difference between the fictional, but still telling, 1971 case and the real 1990s case, is that a lot more[1] information transfer now takes place before the fact. With this transfer of information comes increased responsibility for personal decision-making. Cultural change has meant that the abstract debate about whether individuals should be seen as rational actors has become utterly real.

Risk and rational action

Rational action is directed behaviour to achieve a selected and achievable end. There are three components to this definition: knowledge, selection and behaviour. We have already seen that the question of knowledge is not straightforward. We will not know everything, nor could we hope to. Furthermore, the advice we get may be mistaken, misleading or loaded with criminal intent. Scientists sometimes disagree; and when they do agree, their language may be unintelligible to the person on the street. Sales staff may exaggerate the qualities of their product, and their personal charm may blind us to that even when we know it is going on. Politicians may not highlight the alternatives that exist, and when they do we may not believe them. Channels of communication will cause some distortion of the messages that they carry. With this going on, it is not surprising that best decisions or even merely confident ones may be the exception rather than the rule. And exactly whose selection would it be in the end? When the chief executive decides the

factory must locate to South East Asia, will such a decision somehow belong to the company? Does the decision to have amniocentesis, made between doctor, patient, her partner and *his* mother
(because hers died last year and they have become very close),
belong to the patient or the family? Does it arise out of a session
with a pencil and paper, trying to balance all the alternatives? Or is
it made because it just felt, in the final reckoning, like the right way
to go? Then who takes the action? The chief executive has been
head-hunted to work for a bigger company, the pregnant mother
has been diagnosed with depression but will basically go where she
is led. Before we even begin to start thinking about the relation
between rational action and risk, the complexities are already
enormous. To try to clarify matters, we will first ask if it is only
individual behaviour that can be described in terms of rational
action.

Can organizations act rationally? The immediate answer must
be, 'Of course they can!' Large companies have research departments to provide relevant knowledge about the state of the world.
They have organizational structures that enable discussion and
decision about investment and other options. They have personnel
whose job descriptions require them to follow through on corporate decisions concerning plant closure, site maintenance and waste
disposal. If further evidence were needed, we just have to look at
developments in the law, where corporations all over the world can
be held criminally responsible for negligence or malfeasance, and
we might note the imminent introduction into UK law of the crime
of corporate killing. So, we have to refine the question slightly. If
we ask if all existing organizations can act rationally, the situation
is more complex. The reason is that there is no reliable method for
translating the ranked action preferences of more than two people
into a clear expression of collective preference. This is Kenneth
Arrow's (1963) paradox, and it demands that collective capacity for
consistent decisive action can only be maintained through control
by individuals, whether achieved through clarity of structure or
by some form of dictatorial regime (benign or otherwise). These
considerations apply whether we are dealing with a family, a social
club, a university or a multinational corporation. For legally recognized corporate entities, points of internal responsibility and
agency must be linked to specific individuals, since the collective
entity as rational and responsible agent can only exist (at least,
roughly, within western law) through the individual actions and

contracted responsibilities of its individual officers. So, for an organization to qualify – ontologically speaking – for rational agent status, there has to be an effective chain of command. Similarly for the individual human being, the executive functions of the brain are required to be in good working order (and what is known about what that amounts to is outside the scope of this book) for rational action to be possible.

Now that we have some reason for allowing the individual agent to retain prime position within the discourse of rational action, we can turn to our first connection between rational action and risk: the way we are told about the consequences of possible action. In a famous article, first published in *Science* in 1981, Tversky and Kahneman report on two simple experiments in psychology. In the first, 152 students are put in a hypothetical situation and asked to choose between two alternatives:

> Imagine that the US is preparing for the outbreak of an unusual Asian disease, which is expected to kill 600 people. Two alternative programs to combat the disease have been proposed. Assume that the exact scientific estimates of the consequences of the programs are as follows: if Program A is adopted, 200 people will be saved . . . If Program B is adopted, there is a 1/3 probability that 600 people will be saved, and 2/3 probability that no people will be saved.
>
> (Tversky and Kahneman 1986: 124)

Most of the respondents (72 per cent) chose Program A and the certain saving of 200 people, which was preferred over the three to one shot that 600 might survive. Now, a second set of 155 different students were given the same scenario and asked to choose one of the following: 'If Program C is adopted 400 people will die . . . If Program D is adopted there is a 1/3 probability that nobody will die, and 2/3 probability that 600 people will die'. Of this second set of students, only 22 per cent preferred the certainty of saving 200 lives. The 'same' problem was framed in such a way as to elicit risk-aversion from the first group and risk-seeking from the second group.

The conclusion drawn by Tversky and Kahneman (1986) is that 'the adoption of a decision frame is an ethically significant act' (p. 139), and we may think that those with access to channels of opinion formation – journalists, educators and politicians, for example – should be bound rather more to codes of professional practice that recognize the significance of problem-framing. It must, however, be understood that just as there is an infinity of risks, so there is an infinity of problems capable of being framed differently so as to elicit different responses.[2] We could call for measurement. No matter what the framing of the problem, if there is some way of measuring the benefits of the best outcome and the costs of the worst outcome, then we should be able to avoid some of the uncertainties of subjective response. There is a series of problems here. How do we decide whose consequences are relevant to the decision-maker? The money economy assigns a price to many things, but this may not catch all that we value: the smell of new mown grass or the avoidance of famine in the Sahel, for example. Even setting that to one side and assuming that some combination of measures, like the US dollar or economic utility functions or subjective qualia, could provide a general standard of measurement for outcomes, judgement under uncertainty, with the known values of best and worst outcomes, would still not be concluded. We have to decide on what basis to move from knowledge to decision.

Assuming that our decision will not influence other decisions that may change the anticipated outcomes (which would take us into game theory, about which more in a short while), we may wish to maximize the best possible outcome; we may wish to minimize the damage done under the worst possible outcome; we may want to divide up the consequences and weight some of them, whether in terms of maximizing or minimizing. Aggregation of total utility could be the goal of social welfare decision-making, as could increasing the mean utility for members of the group. Elster puts it as follows:

> . . . facing a choice under uncertainty, does rational-choice theory tell us anything about what we ought to do? The answer is: very little. What it tells us is that we cannot rationally take account of any consequences of an option except the best and the worst. The principle may eliminate some options, but usually the hard choices are left unresolved.
>
> (Elster 1986: 6)

To take just one aspect of that, consider what seems to be quite an attractive general rule for action when we know the details of the best and worst outcomes that may follow from our different options – the maximin principle: maximizing the minimum level of gain across the entire population of those affected by our decision. This principle underlies one of the most significant works of political philosophy written in the twentieth century – John Rawls'

A Theory of Justice (1971) – but has been described by a Nobel
Memorial Prize-winning social scientist as a 'highly irrational
decision rule' with 'absurd practical implications' (Harsanyi 1982:
47). These are illustrated by Brian Barry's (1973) imagined scenario
where there would be 'free or cheap medicine and *ad hoc* subsist-
ence payments provided for those who were very poor, while every-
one else was left to his own devices until his savings had been
exhausted and perhaps those of close relatives too' (pp. 114–15).

Many judgements under uncertainty are taken in circumstances
that are even more complex, where there are competitors who are
also pursuing some of the same scarce resources. This is typically
the case with entrepreneurial and political judgements. Hence the
attention paid to game theory over the last half century. Let me
construct a flawed, but I hope telling, example. In the UK, there are
two main political parties: Labour and Conservative. Both of them
need a policy on joining the European monetary union and adopt-
ing the euro. Let us suppose that each party has done surveys and
worked with focus groups, and thus has some idea of voter reaction
to their stand. An election approaches and both need to publish a
manifesto. Analysing this situation as a game, there are, let us say,
four possible outcomes:

1 Labour commit to the euro and lose two million votes because
   Conservative oppose, trading on economic risk and the preser-
   vation of Britain, and therefore gain two million votes
2 Labour commit to the euro and gain two million votes because
   Conservative prevarication, making them seem weak and hope-
   less even though it is necessary for them to remain in touch with
   the business sector which wants the euro, costs them two million
   votes
3 Labour prevaricate, campaigning as risk-averse but future-
   looking, and gain one million votes because Conservative oppose
   and lose one million votes by appealing to a sense of nationhood
   which cannot be sustained when set against Labour's prudence
4 Labour prevaricate as do the Conservatives and no votes are won
   or lost

In a symmetrical two-handed zero-sum game with both players
facing the same set of decisions, the rational strategy will be to
maximize gains while minimizing losses. But this zero-sum game is
not symmetrical. How will this work? Labour advisers may argue
that their opponents will either prevaricate or oppose. If the

Conservatives prevaricate, Labour either gets two million votes (commit) or nothing (prevaricate). If the Conservatives oppose, Labour either loses two million votes (commit) or gains one million (prevaricate). Thus the rational Labour strategy is to prevaricate, since they have a riskless[3] opportunity to win one million votes depending on how the Conservatives behave.

Since this is not a symmetrical game, unlike the original Prisoner's Dilemma formulated by Albert Tucker in 1950, we need now to do the analysis from the standpoint of Conservative strategy. Their advisers assume that Labour will either commit or prevaricate. If Labour commit, the Conservatives either win two million votes (oppose) or lose two million (prevaricate). If Labour prevaricate, the Conservatives will lose one million votes (oppose) or nothing (prevaricate). We can see that, unlike Labour, the Conservatives do not have a risk-free strategy. Prevarication can gain them nothing and may lose them two million votes. Maximizing their potential gain means opposition, but they may lose one million votes (if Labour prevaricate). They can work out that the maximin strategy for Labour is prevarication, and will decide that their best strategy is opposition, since this maximizes their possible gain and minimizes their possible loss. At this point, however, realizing that their opponents will reason in this way, each will be tempted to change their call to gain advantage, and then at that point the same thinking processes will occur again. This is because this particular game has no Nash[4] equilibrium, no point at which for each side it is not possible to improve whatever the other side does. Stepping out of the game scenario into the real world, the lesson of the analysis may be for Labour to maintain the game until the stakes change, and for the Conservative side to try to alter the potential costs of Labour prevarication, so that they can make a more favourable bet when Labour finally calculate that commitment is less risky than prevarication.

Within game theory work, the situation described above is usually presented in tabular form (see Figure 4.1). The figure is read horizontally and vertically. Labour's strategy and outcome can be seen in the labelling of the horizontal rows, and the figures before the comma in the four outcome cells. Conservative strategy and outcome is seen in the labelling of the vertical columns, and the figures after the commas.

Game theory is a powerful analytical tool for understanding decision-making options in competitive contexts where there will

		Conservative	
		Prevaricate	Oppose
Labour	Commit	+2, –2	–2, +2
	Prevaricate	0, 0	+1, –1

Figure 4.1 A hypothetical game-theory analysis of the UK political decision whether to join the euro

be winners and losers. It consists of rules for constructing and using a complex series of mechanisms, which abstract and expose the complexities of choice made when the effects of the potential decisions of other players have to be taken into account. Thus its potential for examining oligopolistic risk-taking/decision-making – within media organizations, for example – is huge. Two dates might be noted. In 1962, the first paper appeared using game theory to try to advance the understanding of pricing in a competitive market; it took the example of car insurance. Then, in 1994, the game theorists Nash, Harsanyi and Selten won the Nobel Memorial Prize for Economics, by which time game theory work was a part of every discipline in which questions of risk and reward intertwine – that of environmental law, for instance.

The theory of rational action – and of game theory, which is a part of it – can lead to enormously valuable insight into the structure of decisions in the contexts of risk and uncertainty. This body of work, however, may not provide good predictions of decisions taken. Carlo Jaeger and his colleagues, talking about decision theory (a basic form of the rational actor paradigm, and a key site for game theory [Harsanyi 1977: 11]), put it as follows:

> In spite of the highly sophisticated methods in assessing the personal judgements in decision analysis, many studies demonstrate that only a low percentage of decisions follow the rules of normative decision analysis. In other words, people often fail to select the decision option with the highest expected value. It is also yet to be proven that

numerical values and mathematical operations serve as valid representations of verbal reasoning and emotional commitments. As long as sufficient proof for these assumptions is lacking, we cannot know whether actual decision processes are violating the rules of rationality or if the technical skills to understand subjective rationality are underdeveloped.

(Jaeger *et al.* 2001: 81)

Cognitive psychologists have been trying for some time to understand why and how we make the risk decisions that we actually do.

The psychometric paradigm

If attitudes to different kinds of risks are relatively constant within cultures and sub-cultures, we can try to build into any form of rational actor analysis some fairly strong assumptions about what action possibilities are likely and which are not. Is it possible to construct 'cognitive maps of risk attitudes and perceptions' (Slovic 2000: 222)? And would not such cognitive mapping be logically prior to rational action analysis? In 1969, Chauncey Starr attempted to describe what constituted, across some everyday contexts, the general level of acceptable risk. He assumed that we could judge what these levels were by plotting the relationship between risk-information and behaviour. Very roughly, his measure of risk-information was deaths per participant-hour, and his measure of behavioural response to that 'information' was income/expenditure on the activity per participant. He drew three general conclusions. First, risk up to one thousand times greater than levels unacceptable elsewhere were seen as acceptable for voluntary activities such as skiing. Second, the acceptability of a risk (e.g. air travel, electricity, surgery) is roughly proportional to the perceived benefits. Third, the more people take a risk, the more acceptable the risk is (a possible corollary is that reducing numbers of risk-takers make the risk increasingly unacceptable – cf. smoking).

Starr's work laid some of the foundations for what Jaeger *et al.* (2001) have called the 'psychometric school of risk analysis' developed by the work of Paul Slovic and others. Jaeger and his colleagues (2001: 102) suggest that this approach expands the field of risk judgement in four ways:

1 It allows a focus on preference. Enabling, for example, the incorporation into a risk analysis of such apparently sub-optimal

strategies as preferring a solid position with almost no risk of catastrophe, as opposed to considerably higher gain with an increased but still small risk of failure (see Pratt 1964; Simon 1976).

2 As Herbert Simon (1976) has noted, the Olympian view of the rational agent may provide a description of the mind of God, but does not depict very well the cognitive processes of actual decision-makers. Tendencies, leanings and foibles do exist that the rational action approach to risk analysis does not always catch (the mathematical expression of subjective utility functions can sometimes model these effects), and some of these biases are quite important for understanding risk behaviour. In particular, personal experience or another recent involvement with a risk under consideration will tend to co-determine (along with the 'objective' information) judgements, and information which tends to contradict generally held cultural beliefs will tend to be discounted. It should be noted, however, that the 'unrealistic environment' (Gollier 2001: 425) of the tests which can be applied within the psychometric paradigm, combined with a (latent) research design criterion pertaining to a potential for striking results (to increase the chance of impressing funding decision-makers), may lead to some overestimation of the significance of some of the apparent irrationalities.

3 Particular kinds of risk may have a nightmare quality: radiation, asbestos and serial killing, for example. This 'dread' factor has to be fed into rational risk analysis and management where appropriate. Jaeger *et al.* (2001) suggest that this is also the case for perceptions of inequity (relating, for example, to the siting of pylons). When a combination of dread and perceived inequity of treatment is overlaid onto pre-existing suspicions (as was the case when a public outcry prevented a planned investment by Union Carbide in a new plant in Scotland in 1985), cool and detached analysis is unlikely. However, diagnoses of such a syndrome cannot be produced from a distance, as Brian Wynne's work (1982, 1996) on nuclear power in Cumbria demonstrates very well, in its description of the way that extended farming families in Cumbria are locked into the Sellafield economy.

4 Rational actor perspectives on risk do not contend very well with the multiple meanings that may lie behind perceptions of risk. Leaving aside the questions of definition that we considered in the first chapter, Jaeger *et al.* (2001: 105–6) suggest that psychometric

exploration into the cognitive associations of the concept of risk reveals a set of four culturally well-established metaphors that may need to be added as a source of additional enquiry to the more conventional approach to risk. These are risk as the permanent threat embodied in the image of the Sword of Damocles; risk as the uncontrollable and interminable consequences of opening Pandora's Box (in the case of cloning technology, for example); risk as somehow related to an idea of justice, with advantages and disadvantages of a way of life finally coming to rest in balance on Athena's scale; and, finally, risk as something to be desired and triumphed over, as a key to human worth.

Having seen what is claimed for the psychometric paradigm and noted that a part of its appeal is as a corrective to, and enrichment of, the more formal approach to the study of individual risk-taking that we find in the rational action approaches, we can fill out our understanding of the approach by looking more closely at a comparatively recent example.

The study we will examine concerns perceptions of risk of violence from those diagnosed with mental illness. Since 1969, the state of California test for mental patient committal is that potential patients must be shown to be mentally disordered and a danger to themselves or others. Paul Slovic and John Monahan designed a psychometric test to gain insight into three issues:

1 How are judgements of doing harm and dangerousness formed?
2 To what extent are these two concepts equivalent?
3 What level of danger is needed to trigger forced action.

They designed thirty-two hypothetical cases using assemblages from the variables of gender and seven yes–no categories (multiple hospitalizations, delusive, history of assault, angry, impulsive, empathic, socially supported). Thus, one of the cases read as follows:

> TD, a 25 year old male is employed as a bus driver. Records reveal that this is his first admission to a mental hospital. He is not experiencing any delusional beliefs. Relatives report that he has never been assaultive in the past. Among the characteristics of his personality noted in the mental health examination are that he rarely becomes very angry and that he has much empathy or concern for others. TD has many friends and family members to help him with his problems.
> (Slovic and Monahan 1995: 64)

One hundred and ninety-one paid, mostly student, participants in the study were divided into two. Ninety-five were asked to judge each of the thirty-two cases in response to three questions. First, on a zero to ten scale, are they likely to harm someone over the next three years? Second, is the patient dangerous – yes or no? Third, should there be coercion if hospitalization is indicated and they refused? The other ninety-six were asked to perform the same judgements with one variation; on the first question, they were given an extra five micro-percentage options between zero and one.

The results of the study suggest that the concepts of harm and dangerousness are closely correlated, with merely a change in just a few responses required to correlate them exactly. This, perhaps, is not unexpected. What was surprising was that whereas the first group placed 11 per cent of their responses to the first question at either zero or one, the second group, with more gradations in this decile, placed 68 per cent of their responses between zero and one. This clustering of 68 per cent of the responses in the first decile also carried through to judgements of dangerousness, with fewer cases treated as dangerous (18 per cent of the second group found none of the thirty-two cases dangerous, as opposed to just 3 per cent of the first group). Slovic and Monahan statistically analysed the effect of each of the variables on the responses and found that the variable related to history of assault was the most heavily weighted, with anger being the next most significant. Slovic and Monahan subsequently carried out an identical experiment among 137 psychologists, psychiatrists and social workers attending a symposium on law, psychiatry and public policy. They found that the bottom decile clustering also did occur in the second group, but that it did not produce inconsistency of judgements of danger between the two groups: their experience was able to neutralize the response effects deriving from the scale design.

Based on the response effect manipulations we have just examined (and they were re-done, this time with actual rather than hypothetical case studies, some five years later, with similar results[5]), we might be tempted to say that they tell us what we already know. Indeed, the first three conclusions drawn from the study with the students seem to state the blindingly obvious: that 'the judged probability' that a patient will harm someone was strongly related to the judgement that the patient is 'dangerous'; that there is often a 'step function', a line above which a patient is deemed dangerous and potentially harmful and below which a patient was not usually seen as a danger; and if patients were judged to be dangerous, it tended to follow that forced hospital admission would be an option. One way of understanding this aspect of psychometric work is as an exploration of the interrelationship of attitudes, words and concepts. As Wittgenstein (1980: 12) put it, 'Psychological concepts are just everyday concepts.' Since we do not always employ our own familiar concepts in a forensic way, it is necessary for professionals working within these concepts to have a more rigorous appreciation of some of the consequences of their own usages. Here psychometric work can be invaluable. Some of its findings may be obvious, but often they are not. It was not clear, for example, in advance of the experiment, that individuals judged not to be dangerous would sometimes be deemed appropriate for coercive hospital admission if they had a history of prior admissions. Nor could it easily have been concluded in advance that the response scale could have had such an impact on judgements of dangerousness (while this framing effect may be well known among cognitive psychologists, it may be less familiar to social workers, magistrates and fire officers). Finally, would it have been clear that the use of a frequency scale (20 patients out of a hundred with this profile will attack and injure someone within one year of release) leads to higher judgements of risk than would be the case with the use of a probability scale (this patient has a 20 per cent chance of attacking and injuring someone over the twelve months following release) (Slovic and Monahan 2000: 361)?

If we consider the psychometric paradigm to be concerned with the explication of the detailed operations of our cultural and linguistic codes, then a family resemblance to cultural anthropology may be detected. It is possible, therefore, that Mary Douglas's (1999: 220–2) hostility to the psychometric paradigm is at least partly territorial. Nevertheless, she makes six basic criticisms of the approach: the samples are too small; the responses are subjective (but that is surely the point); the test subjects are presented with a limited set of risks; generalization from such artificial situations is unsound; individuals and risks are decontextualized; the personal histories of the test subjects are not taken into account. For Douglas, the psychometric paradigm provides a local assemblage of psychological meanings linked to culturally relevant and specific risks, but provides no research on why some risks rather than others come to emerge as culturally relevant, or on how fear comes to be attached to some risks rather than others.

She finds that the 'castaway' model of psychometric testing may be *de facto* inappropriate to a world in which deciding to take risks is generally a cooperative matter, and she is puzzled about why 'seemingly trite discoveries have been made the basis of worldwide research programmes on the perception of risk?' Perhaps the beginning of a non-partisan response to those three questions might run as follows. First, the question of why some risks rather than others emerge as particularly fearful is capable of being addressed within the psychometric paradigm, as can be seen in work on nuclear waste repositories (Slovic *et al.* 2001), but most work on such cultural change tends to be descriptive of changes that have taken place. We can see this descriptive bias even in work produced under the tutelage of a leading advocate of the psychometric approach (Flynn 2001). The social sciences have not given rise to a generally accepted theory of cultural change (indeed, Douglas herself rejects the strongest contender – evolutionism) and so it may be a little unfair to criticize cognitive psychologists for failing to operate under its auspices. Second, the criticism that the psychometric approach is hyper-individual is only sustainable at a methodological level (in so far as 'isolated' individual subjects are asked questions, and their responses are then aggregated and statistically analysed). In the case of the work with hypothetical mental health case studies examined above, it is clear that the point of the work is to use individual responses as a conduit into the general culture, and that a view of the general culture as highly determinant of individual responses is quite compatible with the psychometric approach (indeed, that is often the point). Third, there is a fairly straightforward answer to why this kind of work may be coming to assume the status of something like normal science: emergent levels of risk-consciousness among formal organizations creates a demand for rigorous exploration of the detailed consequences of their working practices. This applies to biscuit-makers, universities and newspapers. The abstract method of exploring pared-down models of social behaviour, whether done through game theory or the psychometric paradigm, offers rigour, repeatability and testability in various measure. The promise of significance may not always be fulfilled, but there is no plethora of alternatives. The main competition consists of various forms of descriptive account, but the descriptive approach to risk-taking behaviour has come to be dominated by the mass-audience fascination with extreme situations.

The spectacle of high risk contexts

Ranulph Fiennes, in an attempt to reach the North Pole on his own, suffered frostbite to his fingertips, which ultimately he hacksawed off. Part of the description of what he had carefully and with determination planned to do runs as follows:

> Early last year I began training for one of the few polar challenges still to be achieved: an attempt to reach the North Pole solo and un-supported by the direct route of the arctic coastline of North America. I estimated it would take 85 days. For safety I would carry 90 days food. This alone would weigh more than 230 lb, with fuel to melt ice to rehydrate coming to another 60 lb. All additional gear – tent, sleeping bag, mat, cooking kit, rope, axe, shovel, grapnel hook, spare ski, spare clothes, repair kit, medical kit, camera, shot gun, lithium batteries, fluorescent marker poles, paddle – would total another 220 lb: Too much for a single sledge travelling in arctic rubble ice, so I had to use two sledges. This meant every mile gained to the North would mean three travelled on the ground. A one sledge trip is dangerous enough, in that blizzards and whiteouts are common. Perspective is wiped out and ski tracks become invisible. You are in a world of cotton wool, or white night, able to see only your own body: all else is a grey white blur. In such conditions the need to relay sledges involves a potentially lethal risk – once you have parked the first sledge and set off for your final load, you may never find it. At some point you will decide, because of the cold, to return to the first sledge. But it, too, may be impossible to find, you will then die. My schedule took the extra mileage into account. If I could travel North for 10 hours every day for 80 days, with no rest day for injuries, bad weather or watery obstacles, my best progress would be 500 yards a day for the first 3 days, 1.4 miles daily for the next 30 days, 4.5 miles daily until day 58 and then, with a single sledge only, 11 miles daily to the pole.
>
> (Fiennes 2000: 3)

In one sense there is no such thing as a risk context. Since all social contexts can be seen through the lens of risk, there is no objective criterion to differentiate risk contexts from non-risk contexts. Effectively, the latter do not exist within societies that have concern about risk as a basic part of their make-up. Much the same can be said about 'high'-risk contexts. While it may be clear to most of us that what Fiennes is talking about entails a stupefying level of risk, this probably dominant view is not the only one. Fiennes at least thought the risk acceptable.

What is high risk and low risk and for whom, and what that means for the character of the society that we are addressing, are questions which go deep into our culture. Paraphrasing and adapting something Clifford Geertz (1993: 13) said in his seminal essay on 'thick description' – which was a reflection on theory and method and not about risk – one part of contemporary western culture consists of the emerging and established structures of behaviour, knowledge and meaning in terms of which people see and are shown others as risk-takers. What we are trying to look at here is how important that part of our culture is becoming. In pursuit of that question, Stephen Lyng (1990) developed the notion of 'edgework' to describe the personal values – skill, control, superiority – that might lie behind the spread of interest (le Breton 1995) in accomplished participation in potentially dangerous leisure pursuits and 'extreme' sports. David le Breton (1991, 1997) has sought to explain such mortal engagements in terms of personal authentication and the search for moments when the value of being alive is utterly vivid. Anthony Giddens (1991: 126–33) sees the cultivation of risk by individuals as personal experimentation, so that black run skiing, solo climbing and skydiving might be seen as testing and actively extending the limits of the psycho-social security blanket which normally surrounds us.

The picture becomes confused when we consider that extreme pursuits are being colonized by tourist organizations and sports promotion campaigns. Base-jumping is a good example. Base, which is an acronym for Buildings, Antennae, Spans, Earth (i.e. cliffs) – the fixed structures from which parachuting base jumpers launch themselves into the air – has been in existence for around twenty years. A television documentary (Ackerman 2000) was made, in Norway and the UK, exploring this 'underground' activity, in which it 'can take years for someone to find a teacher'. It is true that the documentary team recorded the details of illegal jumps from the Park Lane Hilton, electricity pylons and a monstrous phallic chimney, and that ex-SAS novice-base jumper Terry Forrestal, to whom the programme was dedicated, died from injuries sustained on his eighth jump down a one kilometre sheer face in Norway. However, base-jumping is legal there and is now advertised openly in numerous other places like Yosemite in California and Venezuela's Angel Falls. Anyone with the nerve can sign up to get tuition, probably wearing the latest base-jumping gear from one or two special design outfits in California. Thus there are signs that even a terrifying 'sport' like base-jumping can become normalized, as also illustrated by sky-divers taking part in a celebratory jump from the Kuala Lumpur Petronas towers to celebrate the New Year at midnight on 31 December 2000.

It is doubtful, one might conclude, whether there is any 'high-risk' intentional activity, which, upon emergence, could not become socially mapped, skills-inventoried and Internet-networked. There is, after all that, features journalism to report on the latest extreme activity and inform a public used to feeding off spectacle. Here the focus is likely to be on participant skill, specialized knowledge among a small community, and levels of performance and ability. When, however, the emphasis is not on knowledge, skill and performance, but on the endangerment of self and others, then, at least within western culture, other judgements come more centrally into play.

Take the case of Nigel Wrench, and the practice of unprotected casual sex in the HIV-positive gay community:

> As with drug use, unprotected sex among gay men, particularly among those who are HIV positive, is on the increase almost to the point of normality. It's so normal that personal advertisers and internet chat room users have come up with a name for it. Its called bare backing. Until now it's a practice that has been confined to the anonymous locations of internet chat rooms, personal ads, cruising areas, and London's underground sex club scene. But Nigel Wrench's admission that 'he has had unsafe sex more times than he can remember, often with men whose names I could not tell you now' is a confession which is dangerous for him, given his high profile role as one of the presenters of Radio 4's Prime Time Afternoon News Show PM. He said, 'I am not part of some Aids army out to recruit anyone who comes anywhere near. I simply seek to point out that there is a rational debate to be had. Bare backing can be warm, exciting and involving. We need to debate it. But don't let's start by writing it off as irresponsible and stupid. That frankly is both absurd and dangerous.'
>
> (Wells 2000)

Wrench emphasized that he only ever has sex with other HIV-positive men, but his situated assumption is that if they are in that context with that intent, they are, *ipso facto*, HIV-positive.[6] Wrench argues that it is dangerous to imagine that full responsibility for HIV disclosure can be placed with the positive self, and he implies that the other has to accept the responsibility for being wherever they are. As he puts it, 'It is not good enough to confer on to HIV positive men total responsibility for disclosing their status to their partner . . . it assumes that, in that dark room, every HIV positive man is going to wipe the sweat from his brow and smoke from his eyes and shout above the thumping dance beat: I've got Aids. It's just not a realistic proposition'. The call here is not for policing, but for a reassessment of the notion of innocence. We can infer from his argument that HIV-negative actors in HIV-positive environments cannot be credibly seen as innocent.[7]

There are three points to be made out of this brief excursion into 'high-risk contexts'. First, we do not know enough about them. We are, for example, taken into the worlds of extreme sports through personal web sites, high-octane news stories and more or less accomplished documentary journalism. Professional ethnographers and qualitative sociological researchers do not generally tell us[8] about such activities as hang-gliding, mountaineering, bareback sex communities or white-water rafting. If we try to follow through an everyday view on the increase of risk-taking for pleasure, such as John Vidal's (1999: 2) comment that 'Grannies are parachuting, secretaries are bungee-jumping . . . accountants are big-cliff climbing, doctors . . . are happy to hang-glide, and desk-bound civil servants dream of spending time off doing neck-deep powder-skiing', we find an almost total absence of rigorous inquiry into these activities. What does this mean? Is it that beyond the minor titillations of spectacular or tragic reportage, apart from the participant's personal delight in achieving occasional revelation at what it means to be alive, these activities are relatively marginal? Is this why few people apply to be funded to research them, and why funding councils tend to reject such applications as might be received. There is little research on this,[8] so it is hard to do other than guess. An early conclusion, however, might be that this state of affairs is just a little surprising for societies that are imagined to be obsessed by risk. Perhaps the obsession does not travel so deeply.

Second, what we do know about them comes from participants, very often filtered through the spectacularization processes of the media. An example of this that we considered earlier was the case of Kimberley Bergalis (see Park 1993; see also Diana Fuss's 1993 account of the interpenetration of the Jeffrey Dahmer case with *Silence of the Lambs*). Sometimes we may encounter a serious attempt at objective reportage, as was the case with the *Cutting Edge* television documentary on base jumping. However, even if – unlikely though it might be, especially in the field of high-risk activity – the attempt to seduce an audience through the purveying of spectacle were not dominant, documentary film is not a straight-forward medium.[9]

Third, and to conclude, in societies obsessed by risk one might expect a level of moral panics somewhat greater than appears to be the case. The high-risk contexts we have considered all too briefly give rise either to spectator interest in performance or to concern for the innocent. They do not often seem to lead to widespread and sustained moral panics. Why is it, for example, that concern about resurgent HIV infection among the gay community in the United States and elsewhere is not more widespread? And why does the outrage of affected families following, for example, white-water rafting deaths not lead to more action by politicians, legislators and bureaucrats? If we remind ourselves of the early definition of moral panic provided by Stan Cohen, an answer may become clear:

> A condition, episode, person or group of persons emerges to become defined as a threat to societal values and interests; its nature is presented in a stylised and stereotypical fashion by the mass media; the moral barricades are manned by editors, bishops, politicians and other right thinking people; socially accredited experts pronounce their diagnoses and solutions . . .
>
> (Cohen 1972: 9)

If the threat to the majority arising out of the actions of a minority can be disregarded, then widespread moral panics may not occur or will be short-lived. When they do develop, as has happened in connection with food, childhood and sexuality over the last fifty years, we then have to engage with the question of whom to believe. This brings us to the question of the expert.

Expert Cultures

In this chapter, we raise the question of whom to believe. We know that language, belief and knowledge frame the risks we perceive, and that the way that risks are framed can make a difference to how we respond to them. We also know that the calculative paradigm is not immune to the framing effect. We are, at this point, going to expect that experts will play a major role in the estimation of risk. In fact, we have seen that the development of expert knowledge constitutes one of the core ways in which risks are managed within contemporary western societies. It might also be anticipated that, just like the entrepreneurs, the experts are going to have their own kinds of blinkers, and we can expect some conflicts at the boundaries between the expert field of vision and what lies outside it. We saw that the extrinsic risks from entrepreneurial risk-taking are monitored and borne across the wider array of social institutions, and we will now see that the analogous responsibility for the extrinsic context of expert action within organizations is carried by what has come to be called 'management'. In addition, we have seen that the general documentary media are not a reliable guide to expertise, although they do pay experts to source and validate the illustrated and compelling introductory briefings that are produced to link with issues of the day. We can also anticipate that the approach of cultural anthropologists to expertise will be somewhat suspicious, since expert reportage does not, for them, escape the dilemmas of human motivation or float free of the consequences of social structural context.[1] There are, as we have noted, expert analysts of decision-making processes, imaginative experts in cognitive psychology who can explore decision-preferences in ways that can heuristically support any number of projects, and there are countless models of expert performers who seem to take risks and tell us entertainingly about them for a living. Experts, then, appear to be in the front line of risk analysis. In this chapter, we ask if the concept of the expert is meaningful, what it might mean if experts are not trusted, how experts might be distinguished from managers and consultants and, finally, whether the idea of expert systems ought now to be replaced by that of risk environments.

What is an expert?

John le Carré (1989: 204) wrote, 'I do not like experts . . . When the world is destroyed, it will be destroyed not by its madmen but by the sanity of its experts and the superior ignorance of its bureaucrats.' When Heidegger infamously said to the Club of Bremen in 1949, 'Agriculture is now a mechanized food industry, in essence the same as the manufacturing of corpses in gas chambers and extermination camps, the same as the blockade and starvation of nations, the same as the production of hydrogen bombs' (cited in Rockmore 1995: 150), he displayed astonishing arrogance and insensitivity. But his statement was also a pre-echo of le Carré's. Heidegger's excuse is that he was criticizing the kind of society that would mechanize its food industry.[2] The loss of touch with what is essential to meaningful human existence, an alienation exemplified by the factory farming some think has led to the poisoning of the food we eat, is also revealed, he thought, in nuclear weapons programmes. For Heidegger it is the same syndrome. In his essay on technology, which is a version of that lecture given in Bremen, he talks about a hydroelectric plant on the Rhine:

> The hydroelectric plant is not built into the Rhine River as was the old wooden bridge that joined bank with bank for hundreds of years. Rather the river is dammed up into the power plant. What the river is now, namely, a water power supplier, derives from out of the essence of the power station . . . the energy concealed in nature is unlocked, what is unlocked is transformed, what is transformed is stored up, what is stored up is, in turn, distributed, and what is distributed is switched about ever anew. Unlocking, transforming, storing, distributing and switching about are ways of revealing. But the revealing never simply comes to an end.
>
> (Heidegger 1977: 16)

The revealing of which Heidegger spoke is exemplified in the case of a silversmith forging a sacrificial chalice or of a traditional builder of a boat or a house. Whoever builds or forges such a thing 'reveals what is to be brought forth . . . this revealing gathers together in advance the aspect and the matter of ship or house, with a view to the finished thing envisioned as completed' (Heidegger 1977: 13). The romantic rejection of the continuous processes of modernity inclines Heidegger to a dream of an organic relationship between being and world based on the creative fashioning of small-scale projects that will nestle into the natural world, and whose satisfying completion will be of the project and the life. It is a utopia. It is furthermore a vision which diagnoses technological modernity as diseased. It is critical of both bureaucratic and scientific expertise. The images of the expert that come of out of this line of thinking lead to *Dr. Strangelove* and *Catch-22*, as well as the various scientist-flunkies that work for the super-villains in the world of James Bond. Unless we are prepared to pay the heavy price of rejecting modernity, even a critical account of the expert will be located in the context of the largely irreversible processes that together make up modernity: industrialization, urbanization, bureaucratization, secularization, the emergence of the nation-state, population growth, economic growth, the development of science and technology. This is the general background against which expert cultures have developed.

Experts are recognized for their specialized knowledge and skills, and the ability to apply them in establishing processes or in solving problems within them. Historically, such characters were formed through apprenticeship to a master within a craft guild or equivalent. Elements of those medieval origins remain in science education within the university laboratory and, more generally, in the meritocratic patronage system that is revealed when we discover that leading practitioners in virtually all fields have tended to study with leaders from previous generations.[3] The field of expertise was to some extent consolidated with the sciences and professions when the potential numbers of craft-experts in the heart of the production process was considerably reduced by the advent of mass production from the early twentieth century forward.[4] Although the scientific management that functioned to increase efficiency there might be thought to have functioned to fix one meaning of expert in terms of soulless ergonomics and mechanical system design, so that the birth of the management expert, to the extent that it arose with Henry Ford, can be seen somewhat romantically as a key moment in the history of dehumanization, this perspective is (as are all perspectives) partial. The attention given to the workers by the time and motion engineers was, as the Hawthorne study shows, often psychologically welcomed, and the resulting changes frequently ended up making worksites cleaner, safer and less subject to bullying by charge-hands and foremen. What is more, the markets for mass-produced goods came to require the desire of the 'robotized' workers for the products of the system. Here the dominantly positive image of experts and scientists was exploited as advertisers, especially in the early television age, used images of the expert to confirm the value of what was being sold. Against this background, with post-war expansion into the 1960s fuelled by technological advances such as television, the transistor and the jet engine, the place of the expert in pure research, applied development, management support and political consultancy – underpinned by burgeoning professional associations – seemed secure.

During the 1950s, a set of gargantuan processes was already in train. They would soon provide new contexts for the idea of the expert, and would often come to frame that figure in terms of suspicion rather than confidence. Cold War rivalries between the United States and the Soviet Union led to the creation of surveillance organizations like the FBI and KGB, which saw experts as a risk of defection and betrayal. Population growth, fast industrialization and technological innovation would begin to reveal their environmental consequences; and it would be experts who would blow the whistle – against themselves, as it were. Nuclear technology, still in its infancy but irrevocably associated with Hiroshima and Nagasaki, began to be widely demonized as hubristic flirtation with mass destruction by experts. The following passage from Maarten Hajer's fine discussion of environmentalism summarizes this welling change of atmosphere as follows:

> First of all there was a growing fear of industrial catastrophes. The increase in the scale and complexity of industrial production, in which professional experts had to control increasingly dangerous and complex processes, was met by a growing suspicion of the expert. Professionalism, originally meant as one of the major instruments for perfectibility, came to be distrusted. Secondly ... the environmental movement of the 1970s ... came to the fore through its stringent anti-consumerism, its anti-alienation attitude, its commitment to democratisation, and its protest against what Galtung called 'the colonisation of the future'. It indicated that the radical environmentalism of the

1970s should be seen as part of a larger critique of the process of
modernisation and rationalisation. It was, as Suzanne Berger so nicely
put it, directed 'not against the failure of state and society to provide
for economic growth, but against their all-too-considerable success in
having done so, and against the price of this success'. This general
mistrust was reinforced by the fact that the more educated public now
also had easier cognitive access to the possibility of systemic failure
and could more easily understand the particular nature of systemic
irrationalities. On top of all of this there was a growing frustration with
the perceived insensitivity of the 'new class' of experts and technocrats
to the spheres of the human life-world ... People felt that they had
become entangled in all kinds of organisational systems that were
entirely beyond their control.

(Hajer 1995: 87–8)

There is one further,[5] highly significant and coeval development
that needs to be explored to complete our picture. It relates to the
creation of experts and fields of expertise by legislation. It, too, can
carry certain negative meanings. Jurgen Habermas has suggested
that the creation of legally empowered administrative offices in the
areas of family, education and social welfare has been part of what
he calls the 'colonization of the lifeworld' (Habermas 1987: 332–73;
Outhwaite 1994: 82–108). The timing of this process of lifeworld
rationalization has been unfortunate. It created expert worlds of,
inter alia, developmental psychologists, social workers and edu-
cational counsellors, together with the professional cadres within
the law and administration to support them, and the dedicated
political lobbyists representing – quite properly – the interests
served by all these agents. It did this, however, at a time when confidence in expertise generally was falling away, and when an
enhanced risk sensitivity was emerging. Habermas wrote:

The further the structural components of the lifeworld and the processes that contribute to maintaining them get differentiated, the more
interaction contexts come under control of rationally motivated
mutual understanding, that is, of consensus formation that rests in the
end on the authority of the better argument.

(cited in Outhwaite 1994: 87)

However, what he did not go on to say, with any real clarity,[6] was
that the 'better argument' would have been judged as such at least
in part because it reflected the background cultural ambience of
the time (from the perspective in which we are interested: confidence deficit and risk sensitivity). The transposition of that 'better'

argument into an institutional framework can contribute towards a confirming imposition in practice of those background assumptions onto the lifeworlds of the affected.

Mistrust

It might appear remarkable after all the above that we still seem to place some trust in expertise. This works in four ways. We are prepared to trust experts whom we know and on whom we have previously relied (and lived to tell the tale). We will define an expert as someone on whom we would be prepared to rely. We will trust systems that have been constructed by experts and that are necessary to us and seem mostly to work. Finally, we have no alternative: if we travel, buy food, have bank accounts, undergo tests at the hospital, keep children in school and use the electricity at home, we are reliant on expertise. Now, all of this concerns our implicit and explicit grants of trust to the people and with respect to the things around us. It is linked umbilically to the agent-centred view of the social world. If, however, we have no alternative but to place trust in certain institutions, probably the agent-centred view is not going to tell us very much that is interesting here. It is when we do have alternatives that agency becomes interesting.[7] When we don't have any choice, we need to look at the structures to see whether this is and why this is the case. We will find that trust is a precondition of social life, but that some forms of it may be threatened within the public sphere, and this does have implications for how we deal with experts and risk.

First, let us look at two classic arguments that tell us we have no alternative but to bestow some level of trust on the systems and people around us. The first is from Harold Garfinkel's 1963 publication, 'A conception of and experiments with "trust" as a condition of stable concerted actions'. Garfinkel wanted to know what it is that we have to place our trust in so that we can continue to have perfectly ordinary interactions, and continue to live our ordinary everyday lives without too many disruptions. He thought that we place our trust in whatever it is that implicitly promises to reproduce the ordinary world of everyday living. He also saw that the giving of this trust (not intentionally or as a conscious agent in this respect) actually contributes to making the social order in which we are trusting. He thought that we place trust in an ensemble of which we ourselves are a part. In other words, that we place our trust in the social milieu at the same time as we place trust in ourselves as competent members of that same social environment. For Garfinkel, we place our trust in the invariant features of the inter-action context and in the ability of ourselves and others to negoti-ate them. Through experimentation, he thought it was possible to confirm what these invariants are. When he got his students to role-play being lodgers in their own homes, they reported back that the consequent level of argument and disruption was spectacular. Garfinkel's 'experiments' confirmed for him that we trust through a paradoxical complicity that is both unwitting and highly skilled. Transferring from the world of experiment to that of routine every-day life, Garfinkel's work showed that the introduction of risk concerns over time – food allergies, travelling home alone, un-employment – simply add to the background structure of inter-actional invariants that are unwittingly acknowledged and negotiated by the competent interactants once they become fixed. The same is true with regard to any interactional invariants about system reliability and expertise.

Niklas Luhmann's disagreement with the social action paradigm is more explicit than Garfinkel's. He criticized modern sociology for its predominant tendency, as he saw it, to analyse social organizations in terms of rational action. He thought that individual rationality should be subsumed under system functioning rather than the other way around. Luhmann wrote as follows:

> Trust, in the broadest sense of confidence in one's expectations, is a basic fact of social life. In many situations, of course, man can choose in certain respects whether or not to bestow trust. But a complete absence of trust would prevent him even from getting up in the morn-ing. He would be prey to a vague sense of dread, to paralysing fears. He would not even be capable of formulating definite *distrust* and making that a basis for precautionary measures, since this would pre-suppose trust in other directions. Anything and everything would be possible. Such abrupt confrontation with the complexity of the world at its most extreme is beyond human endurance.
>
> (Luhmann 1979: 3)

Trust, for Luhmann, is a key functional requirement for the management of complexity. If we turn a neo-Kantian eye on the mass of information that is presented to us when we walk down a city street, how do we make that mass of input manageable? For Luhmann, we manage that complexity through trusting in the stability of the environment with singular exceptions like the traffic.[8] It is those exceptions on which attention is focused. Trust, then, implies some knowledge, and it also entails the taking of risks – that the paving slabs are even, for example. Here it can be seen that trusting is not a simple matter of information processing. It is actually a matter of defining the immediate future: 'one engages in action as though there were only certain possibilities in the future'. There is no real alternative, merely putting in an appearance in any social context exposes us to risk. If we cannot trust in any social context, there is an enormous problem. But seeing this also shows us that, to the extent we are able to trust, we not only reduce complexity, we also build up greater possibilities for action. Thus trust is not merely a risk, it is also an investment. It is a precondition of the creation of social capital (Tonkiss 2000). As Francis Fukuyama put it in a lecture following the 1996 US election:

> When you dissect what gives people the ability to work together, to trust one another in a group or association or business, you see that social capital is the sharing of certain norms or values concerned with truth-telling, honesty, reliability and the like, and it would seem to be commonsensical that if you have a society in which people trust each other spontaneously you are going to be more efficient than in a society where people distrust each other.
>
> (Fukuyama 1996: 1)

Reciprocal trust enables new ways of behaving. There are, however, limits to what this interpersonal trust can achieve: 'modern differentiated social orders are much too complex for the social trust essential to ordinary living to be created solely by this type of orientation towards persons' (Luhmann 1979: 7). What Luhmann thinks is required is 'system trust'. System trust – in money, in the democratic process, in professionally accredited testimony – has been for Luhmann one of the great civilizing processes.

Now, risk consciousness does not mean abandonment of trust. It means more or less focused distrust. The less focused the distrust, the more complex the world. More information is needed, and less information becomes dependable. Distrust is more demanding than trust, reducing possibilities for learning and adaptation. As Luhmann (1979) puts it, 'Relatively, trust is the easier option, and for this reason there is a strong incentive to begin a relationship with trust' (p. 12). This applies whether the relationship is to another social actor or to a system. It also applies within a risk-conscious society. It is an empirical question whether mutterings and moanings about the inefficiencies of a system, and even lay complaints about its potential dangers, transform system trust into the considerable complications of system distrust.

While both Garfinkel and Luhmann conclude that trust is a pre-condition for interactional competence and social functioning, Adam Seligman does not focus on the necessity of trust. He considers that some forms of it have become almost impossible. Seligman agrees that it is a precondition of social relationships that a level of confidence and familiarity in our social systems should exist. Both Garfinkel and Luhmann refer to this as trust. Seligman thinks this is a precondition of trust. But unlike Giddens, who advocated active trust prior to the formation of clear structures, Seligman thinks that trust is granted to enable flexibility of performance within structures that are established. It is linked to friendship and the latitude that friends grant to each other. In the modern world, with the inexorable development of the division of labour as represented by the growth of fields of expertise, such trust is harder to grant. Globalization and other forms of social change dissolve the conditions for confidence and familiarity on which such trust can be based. Increasing political, economic, cultural and environmental pressures lead to systemic relationships founded not on familiarity and confidence-based trust, but on control, specification and the amelioration of mistrust through monitoring. Seligman (1997) thus draws a distinction between the public and private spheres: 'We are thus identifying with the public realm the phenomenon of confidence in systematically enforced expectations, and the private with those of trust, individual agency and a space for the negotiation of role expectations' (p. 148).[9] The consequence of this is a move from autonomous and self-regulating experts to technically skilled functionaries operating within a well-specified context – in other words, to expert systems.

Experts *vs* managers

Jurgen Habermas (1996), in his huge, specialized and closely argued text *Between Facts and Norms*, provides an analysis of the law within the context of the history of rationalization. He is a critic of the over-rationalization of the lifeworld. He points to a key example when discussing the systems of interpretation imposed on judges by the judicial system. A simple view of the matter shows expert witnesses translating scientific testimony into terms a 'reasonable person' might understand – into lay terms, in other words. For Habermas, however, the process is more elaborate than this:

> Procedural principles and maxims of interpretation that are constitutive for the role and practice of impartial adjudication . . . are meant to ensure the independence of the judiciary, constraints on individual discretion, respect for the integrity of the disputing parties, the written justification and official signing of the judgement, its neutrality, and so on. *Professionally proven standards* are meant to guarantee the objectivity of the judgement and its openness to . . . review.
>
> (Habermas 1996: 224)

This professional specification of objectivity does not mean that the judge is neutral. Judges have 'an unavoidable background understanding of society', an implicit social vision. Habermas cites Henry Steiner's (1987) *Moral Argument and Social Vision in the Courts* as follows:

> By social vision . . . I mean conceptions of courts about society (its socio-economic structure, patterns of social interaction, moral goals and political ideologies), about social actors (their character, behaviour, and capacities), and about accidents (their causes, volume and toll). The concept then includes courts' understandings about matters as varied as the incidence and social costs of accidents, the operation of market pricing mechanisms, the capacity of individuals for prudent behaviour, the bureaucratic rationality of business forms, the effects of standard clauses in contracts, and ideologies of growth or distribution in the nineteenth century or today. Social vision embraces not only empirical observations (the number of auto accidents), but also evaluative characterisations of events (the absence of free choice in a given context) and feelings of disapproval or empathy towards what is described (a 'sharp' bargain, or a 'tragic' loss).
>
> (Habermas 1996: 392–3)

The judge in the courtroom is a model for overarching understanding of complex sites with multiple expert interfaces. But it is neither simple nor unproblematic. The alternative model is also drawn from the law – the brief: the establishment of terms of reference, including a statement of general values and a set of specific objectives to be achieved within a given period. The brief tries to draw everything relevant to the surface and lock it in a tight protocol for action. The judicial model is based on trust, while the legal one begins from control. In contemporary economic life, the legal model is the norm (and Fukuyama may be something of an idealist if he believes that the extended trust relations in contemporary economies are not ultimately subordinate to contractual law, and are not mostly hedged by the checks and balances of monitoring and required reporting relationships). It dominates the contractual or quasi-contractual relationships entered into by consultants, managers and even governments.

We have little sociological or anthropological data on the relative efficacy of this model, since researchers, when they can gain access, will generally be required to work within the agreed terms of the organization. To model the oversight of expertise across the alternative principles of trust (professional autonomy) and mistrust (system specification), we can try to use the following, compiled by Habermas (1996: 405) in his attempt to understand the significance of the development of welfare regulation over the last fifty years:[10] The two lists reveal the default interpretive principles applied to business disputes fifty years ago contrasted with those applied today.

The liberal view	*Today's view*
Unique	Statistical
Individual, personal	Category, impersonal
Concrete, anecdotal	Generalized, purged of detail
Occasional, random	Recurrent, systemic
Isolated conduct	Part of an activity
Unforeseeable	Predictable
(in the particular)	(in the aggregate)
Wait and see, fatalism	Manageable, planning through
	insurance and regulation

The left-hand side provides a view of, for example, an individual mental health case seen from the perspective of the family. The right-hand side can give us a view of the same case from the standpoint of the administration of a contemporary healthcare system. The more variation (trust and autonomy) allowed to individual cases, the more difficult planning and management become: 'From this point of view, the administration and private actors are involved in a zero-sum game: what the one gains in competence the other loses' (Habermas 1996: 406). It is possible that the relation between management and expertise can be recursively analysed using this model, in which case it might move towards something like the following speculative contrast between the perspectives of the specialist and the chief executive officer (CEO):

Expert	CEO
Specific causal mechanisms	Assignment of priority
Solution proposal	Assessment of risk
Individual fault analysis	Personnel analysis
Cost estimate	Cost allocation
Specific authority	Systemic responsibility
Isolated problems	Part of a syndrome
Unforeseeable	Predictable
(in the particular)	(in the aggregate)
Leave it to us	Plan, regulate, monitor

Merely playing through this thought experiment from the hypothetical standpoint of an actor within a systemic environment (a large government department or a multinational corporation, for example) throws the opposition between expertise/trust and management/system into sharp relief.[11] But now let us briefly consider a case study to reach one or two tentative conclusions.

The 1986 *Challenger* launch

The National Aeronautics and Space Administration (NASA) has been a household name in the West, synonymous with expertise, quality, technological research and success. It probably sustained that reputation through the 1980s, at least in the mind of Christa McAuliffe's mother. She had been impressed by the sight of the shuttle on its platform the night before the launch, and had been puzzled that NASA personnel apparently could not deliver a portable drill with a working battery to fix a problem with a hatch door. Her daughter was going to be the first teacher in space, and this was the third time the flight had been called off.

The shuttle programme had its origins in the late 1960s when it was decided that the core of NASA's strategy would be based on the construction of an Earth-orbiting space station[12] serviced by a shuttle vehicle. The shuttle was the logical priority. Following Nixon's final decision on NASA's future strategy, it took eleven years for the first live shuttle to be launched, on 12 April 1981. Another twenty-three were successfully launched over the next five years. All of them were launched with the design feature that was held responsible for the accident on 28 January 1986, which killed the seven astronauts. Back in 1973, a decision had to be made whether to go for a modular design for the rocket boosters, which meant they would be fabricated and transported in stages and then sealed together, or a monolithic design. The bids for the segmented design were superior, and Morton Thiokol won the tender. A critical part of the design was the seal between the segments of these huge cylindrical booster rockets. This was achieved by two rubber rings called the primary and secondary O rings. These sealing rings failed, thus causing the accident. The monitoring detail from the accident record represents state-of-the-art forensic engineering:

> . . . the Solid Rocket Boosters were increasing their thrust when the first flickering flame appeared on the right Solid Rocket Booster in the area of the aft field joint. This first very small flame was detected on image enhanced film at 58.788 seconds into the flight. It appeared to originate at about 305 degrees around the booster circumference at or near the aft field joint. One film frame later from the same camera, the flame was visible without image enhancement. It grew into a continuous well-defined plume at 59.262 seconds. At about the same time (60 seconds), telemetry showed a pressure differential between the chamber pressures in the right and left boosters. The right booster chamber pressure was lower, confirming the growing leak in the area of the field joint. As the flame plume increased in size, it was deflected rearward by the aerodynamic slipstream and circumferentially by the protruding structure of the upper ring attaching the booster to the External Tank. These deflections directed the flame plume onto the surface of the External Tank. This sequence of flame spreading is confirmed by analysis of the recovered wreckage. The growing flame also impinged on the strut attaching the Solid Rocket Booster to the External Tank. The first visual indication that swirling flame from the right Solid Rocket Booster breached the External Tank was at 64.660 seconds when there was an abrupt change in the shape and colour of the plume. This indicated that it was mixing with leaking hydrogen from the External Tank. Telemetered changes in the hydrogen tank pressurization confirmed the leak. Within 45 milliseconds of the breach of the External Tank, a bright sustained glow developed on the black-tiled underside of the Challenger between it and the External Tank. Beginning at about 72 seconds, a series of events occurred extremely rapidly that terminated the flight.
>
> (Rogers 1986: 19–20)

This termination occurred less than sixteen hours after the engineering experts at Morton Thiokol had told NASA not to launch because the cold temperature would mean that the O rings would not seal and the result would be catastrophe. A Presidential Commission was set up to find out what exactly happened.

In essence, NASA was under tremendous budgetary and political pressure to deliver a commercial space shuttle programme, to move from twenty-four flights over five years to twenty-four flights a year (Vaughan 1996: 32). They were being forced to increase continuously the output of this colossal expert system, of this assemblage of expert systems, at the same time as having their budgets seriously cut. The previous flight had been put back six times before launch and now *Challenger*, having already been postponed three times, was forecast for launch in temperatures below 0° C. This was unusual in Florida and had never happened before for a shuttle launch. The previous coldest launch temperature was 53° F (12°C), and after that launch the recovered solid rocket boosters (SRB) showed signs of burn and erosion at the O rings. This was not the first sign of such damage, but, according to the Thiokol engineers, primarily responsible for this part of the operation, it had been by far the worst. Following that discovery by the engineers in 1985, they had campaigned within Morton Thiokol to try to get something done about the problem. For them, the cold rings meant poor sealing and the whole problem meant bad design. They were allowed to investigate, but given no resources. Thus no significant new information was available in January 1986. There was just the evidence of erosion at the 53° F launch. Under take-off pressures the whole SRB assembly would flex, and the O rings had to do a job for which they were not specifically designed, expanding because of their innate pliability to fill the small gap created before it could be breached by leaking hot gases. The concern was that below 53° F the minimum functional level of pliability would be lost. But there were no data. Morton Thiokol did not devote sufficient resources to investigating the problem from 1985, partly because it was not a new problem. It had been recognized as a possible risk back in 1973 when discussions were taking place about segmented or monolithic rocket boosters. At that time, and ever since, it had been seen by both NASA and Thiokol as an acceptable risk. Diane Vaughan, in a superb piece of social science, argues convincingly that the acceptance of this risk between 1981 and 1984 constituted a process of normalization of deviance that tolerated seven of the nine launches in 1985 showing signs of O ring erosion. The third of these flights had resulted in a launch constraint requiring the fault to be fixed, but this technical flight embargo was thereafter waived for each subsequent launch.

It was into this context that the Thiokol engineers advanced.

They persuaded their company to recommend postponement because of the temperature forecast. It was going to be below zero. NASA would be very unhappy, but they were informed in a forty-five minute telephone conference. A second telephone conference call between NASA and Thiokol was arranged two hours later, with the participation of key actors. Thiokol gave a relatively unprepared presentation, but the argument was clear. Mulloy, the NASA manager on the SRB project, Lovingood, deputy manager of the Shuttle Projects Office, and George Hardy, deputy director of science and engineering at Marshall Space Center, combined to reflect pressure back at Thiokol. This erosion had been known about for a long time. Established temperature launch criteria were not being breached. Although there had been blow-back in cold conditions, it had also been seen at room temperature.

Morton Thiokol's vice-president for space booster programmes had clearly recommended no launch, but now there came a request for an off-line caucus at Thiokol. During that caucus, Jerald Mason, senior vice-president of Thiokol, re-rehearsed the NASA response: the lack of data, the previous record, the standing decision to allow the O ring design as acceptable risk, the poor and contradictory evidence of the increased risk of colder temperatures, the existence of two seals so that if one did not seal the other one would, and tests on a smaller scale that had been done below freezing point which showed no blow-back. He was going to be centrally involved in Thiokol's pitch for renewal of their $1 billion contract with NASA, and saw his responsibility as providing clear management leadership.[13] Jack Kapp, the engineering supervisor over Thiokol's SRB engineers who was part of the caucus, reflected later, 'It was obvious to me that based on what he had seen and heard, Jerry then, for whatever reason, wanted to fire' (cited in Vaughan 1996: 316). As part of his discussion, Mason asked for 'a management decision', and when one of the senior managers hesitated, Mason asked for him 'to take off his engineering hat and put on his management hat' (ibid.). As a microcosm of the general interface between experts and managers, the scenario is classic.

The four senior managers overruled the engineers and affirmed it was clear to launch. Thiokol was not asked for its rationale for decision reversal, merely to confirm it in writing, and the whole matter was closed down without being adequately reported upwards. The director of Marshall Space Flight Centre, Bill Lucas, was not fully briefed on the teleconference outcome, in part because at 5 am on launch day when such a briefing would have been possible, the O ring problem had been superseded by the icicles on the launch structure problem. Had Lucas wanted to report the matter further up, the next step was the chief of the Office of Space Flight, Jesse Moore. However, according to one Marshall engineer, such people were not 'in the seat of understanding' (Vaughan 1996: 261). Also looking further upward for answers was not going to do much when the top NASA administrator was on leave of absence, and his acting replacement was a policy analyst. The Presidential Commission stayed within blinkers, it did not ruminate on the tectonic interface between management and expert. It found that NASA decision procedures were flawed, that imposing and removing launch constraints routinely happened two levels below executive responsibility, and that Thiokol reversed its no launch recommendation in response to pressure. These findings themselves are within system, just as, strictly speaking, both NASA and Morton Thiokol (whose contract was renewed) were.

For the wider relevance of the *Challenger* accident, however, the best place to turn is Chapter 10 of Diane Vaughan's (1996) monumental book. She makes *inter alia* the following points (which I will annotate to a small extent):

- Technical specifications were perversely used against their original intention.
- Corrective technical measures create new possibilities for failure (experts have to carry responsibility for these first two points).
- The routine complexities of engineering decision-making were hidden from the public (this has generally been the case with expert systems, and was probably a precondition of trust in them; but the context is changing and routine warnings coupled with extensive available information have come to be the norm).
- The normal[14] working within expert systems requires anomalies to be ignored until there is an unavoidable build-up.[15]
- The middle managers got the blame, while the remote elites were exonerated (as Mary Douglas's work on culpability and culture might lead us to appreciate).
- NASA's top management promoted a utopian dream of routine space flight.
- The culture of success tended to prevent teams warning of potential danger (as Vaughan points out, the rational analysis of risk has traditionally operated at the level of the organization, and it

needs routinely to be extended to the participants within, not simply in terms of the organizational goals, but also in terms of the stakes for the participants themselves).
• Routine organizational working more or less requires an attitude of bounded rationality (blinkers or tunnel vision as I have called it earlier) from its participants.
• Even when all possible efforts are made to understand a complex socio-technical event, the explanation produced will still be too simple.

As we look through these points, it is tempting to suggest that the distinction between management and expert is itself a cultural construction, that the roles may be separable, but actually they are entirely implicated with each other. In practice, this may often be the case, but they very regularly separated out, and the roles can be made quite clear when necessary, and they frequently are. Jerald Mason's management of the off-line caucus illustrates that as clearly as can be. Thus Vaughan concludes her chapter with some feeling, saying:

> The lingering uncertainty in the social control of risky technology is how to control the institutional forces that generate competition and scarcity and the powerful leaders who, in response, establish goals and allocate resources, using and abusing high-risk technical systems.
>
> (Vaughan 1996: 422)

Expert systems or risk environments?

Both the *Challenger* case and that of the Bhopal accident warn us against using Fukuyama's optimistic conception of trust as an ideal against which to measure organizational life. Organizations are realms of more or less systematically enforced expectations. An 'expert' trying to challenge the system of which he or she is a part will not be trusted. The word 'expert' is in effect a collective noun, and the notion of an expert system is pleonastic, an expert outside of a systemic context is a contradiction in terms. Can the term 'expert system' be made meaningful or should it be forgotten, perhaps to be replaced by the idea of risk environments (Giddens 1991: 109–43)? To the extent that the concept of the expert system takes us into the detail of the particular environment and its norms and procedures, its spirit needs to be retained. As Vaughan (1996) says, at the end of her book, 'explanation lies in the details'. Expert system is, then, an investigator's concept. The starting point of an inquiry. What are the rules and how do they interlock? That compound question is asked by both the computer analyst and the accident investigator. Discovering what happened and discovering the system, and some of its risks, take place at the same time. The concept of the expert system suggests that many risks reveal themselves during design. Their prior identification is something we can expect from the expert, who thus holds a pivotal position in the 'risk society'. But experts do not automatically constitute systems we can trust. In this context, the precondition of some existential security is education, and a partial refusal to be entirely subordinated to alien technology.

Risk Society?

Do we live in a risk society?[1] This is an important question to ask, but not one which is capable of a straight answer. In this last chapter, I will try to explore this conundrum, and will conclude with a short statement of five key theses for understanding risk in the contemporary era.

From invisible risks to global flows

In framing the risks that confront us, does our language, belief and knowledge reflect a world that is just plain riskier than it ever was before? Do we now accept, whether as consumers, employees, pension fund contributors, parents, sportswomen, teachers or revellers, that our duty of care to ourselves has become more demanding? Are we more suspicious about the motives or competence of people who appear at the door, answer our telephone inquiries, respond to questions in Parliament, or talk to us about the operation our son is going to have? What constitutes our form of tunnel vision? Who is thinking outside of it, and what are the forces seeking to narrow or widen our focus? Whom can we trust? Is there a public record worthy of that description? Could we really expect there to be one, if every statement is locked to its time, place and the interests it serves? How can we fly above all this and get a view of the overall terrain? It was because it promised to give such a view to us, that the work of Ulrich Beck created a great deal of interest.

Beck thinks we have been eye witnesses to a break within modernity. His subject is the shift from classical industrial society to a new self-endangering civilization, which he calls second

modernity or risk socie...
with one particular event...

> ... questions of periodizat...
> basic happened in the 1960s...
> state reform, education ref...
> emergence of the language of...
> technology were occasioned by...
> promise the collective suicide of...
> beginning of an environmental n...
> ment supported by scientists and e...
> colleagues. We can choose to pi...
> developments to mark the line be...
> reflexive risk modernity, but there ar...   ...ry hard,
> in the face of such complex changes, t...   ...o a modal event
> which fully signifies a clear cut betwee...   ...and second modernity.
>
> (Beck in Boyne 2001: 63)

Escalating risks have shaken progress and transformed politics. By risks, Beck starts with two things. First, he means the physical hazards that can destroy life – radioactivity, toxins, pollutants – invisible dangers that threaten us all. Bhopal and Chernobyl are two obvious cases. These risks threaten us on a giant scale. They are no longer the side-effects of progress, they are progress. Environmentalists say that politicians are not really concerned with environmental quality and ecological value, only quantity and money, that they have insufficient grasp of how important the language of risk and safety has become within the conscience collective. Second, he means that there are social and cultural insecurities: sex, work, the street, marriage, childhood – where do we look to find an area of social life that is immune to the miasma of risk and uncertainty?

This 'second' modernity has brought a new politics. The potency of recent historical driving forces – bourgeoisie, working class, the masses, electorates, the nation-state, superpowers, information technology – has diminished. Nations cannot deal effectively with international risk (within the European Union, consider immigration or the barely admitted contradiction between the Common Agricultural Policy and the commitment to 'widening and deepening'), with global division of labour, with atmospheric pollution. What are the consequences of micro-technology – sack the clerical labour force? Is the thirty-year move from typing pools to call centres part of what Beck calls the 'Brazilianization of the West?'

untry such as Brazil, those who depend
full-time work represent only a minority of
tive population; the majority earn their living in
conditions. People are travelling vendors, small
craft-workers, offer all kinds of personal service, or shuttle
forth between different fields of activity, forms of employ-
t or training. As new developments show in the so-called highly
developed economies, this nomadic 'multi-activity' – until now mainly
a feature of female labour in the West – is not a premodern relic but a
rapidly spreading variant in the late work-societies, where attractive,
highly-skilled and well-paid full-time employment is on its way out.

(Beck 2000: 1–2)

Market logics, techno-logics, socio-logics appear to have control. It
was, of course, always like this. Now, however, there is more reflexive awareness. The active thought that our social and sub-social
systems should be for us rather than over us is beginning to
emerge. If risk society is reflexive modernity, then we are in the
first stage after this reflexive turn, without certainty of what lies
in store. Sociological critique, in this scenario, was never so
important.

We have to be careful not to think of this as a simple before and
after situation. Although Beck argues that western society has
moved over a period of around 400 years from pre-modernity
through classical modernity to reflexive modernity, and while he is
saying that modernity in the classical sense means much the same
as industrial society, these notions are best seen as ideal types. They
are analytic constructions that we use to help us understand the
actual case that we are examining. Thus the world in which we live
is still illuminated by the notion of industrial society, although the
light provided by this idea is just a little less penetrating than it was.
Now perhaps the notion of risk society/reflexive modernity is
beginning to shine more brightly over the whole scene and to
highlight forms within it which only recently emerged. So, one key
problematic of industrial society is the distribution of wealth and
the legitimation and amelioration of inequality. In risk society, we
must add the distribution and amelioration of harm. In reflexive
modernity, the social production of wealth is systematically accompanied by the social production of risks. Wealth and power are
defining concepts of classical modernity, but the signature concepts
of reflexive modernity are risk and uncertainty. Industrial society
was always a risky place, but there has been a step change. The

symptomatic risks of
Atomic plants are neit
dent is not just an acc
those not yet born and t
calculate the consequ
inaugurated at Los Ala
serious scientific hypot
atmosphere, means tha
come to be a dominant

The globalization of
about in reflexive mode
are metamorphosing. U
feudal sex roles of me
renegotiated; the bound

ring with familiar forms or pluralized underemployment (government departments adopt famine-relief-type schemes scratching at
the syndrome of underinvestment and overexpectation with the
needle of targeted funding initiatives, which promise part-time jobs
and short-term contracts); the scepticism and demand for evidence
inherent within science has been turned onto both the founding
assumptions of science itself (questions of ontology, ethics, entitle-
ment, scope, ownership) and its products (for example, nuclear and
biotechnological hazards); the ubiquity of the language and (albeit
ritual) process of modern democracy throws into relief the near-
pathological immunity from social shaping that has characterized
the areas of business, science and technology, major forces that
incline our societies in ways over which even presidents and prime
ministers have had relatively little say. Notions of class, family,
work, science, progress, democracy 'crumble and disintegrate in the
reflexivity of modernization' (Beck 1992: 14). The promise of
certain and willed direction that comes with single-issue campaigning, identity politics and social movements may present such relief
in these overall circumstances that it should only be a surprise that
they have not gained more in importance.

We have already noted the burdens of risk assessment that new
levels of information and choice may impose on us. For Beck, this
has the effect of throwing individuals more onto their own
resources, a thesis he refers to as *individualization*. With the scep-
tical spirit of scientific critique now pointed at science itself
(another mode of *reflexive* modernization), the lay public is invited
by the media to sit in judgement upon expertise and to engage in

...unter-expertise. As Claus Offe (1992)
...rlier example of amniocentesis, this loss
...oint places a serious burden of risk assess-
...he end, the public, comprising citizens and lay
... not only on practical self-help, but also on the
...gnitive interpretation of the situation, along with the
...us consequent risks of myth formation [and] panic
... (p. 68). This implication of Beck's perspective is drawn
...though skeletally, into a critique by Habermas, who, while
...dly approving of the risk society thesis, was critical of the lack
of an intersubjective micro-perspective in Beck's thinking. He
wrote: 'what these subjects [of reflexive modernity] must perform
is the kind of moral and existential self-reflection that is not
possible without the one taking up the perspective of the other'
(Habermas 1992: 199). Habermas is saying here that Beck will
have no significant critique of risk society unless he draws it from
the intersubjective lifeworlds of the actors who populate it. But
Habermas could not easily sharpen his critique into a cutting tool,
since the acute version of his objection is that it does not feed
directly from the actual and rigorously documented lifeworld
experiences of human beings, and this would have applied just as
much to his own perspective. So Beck's claim that his work has a
'profound intersubjective dimension' was an easy response to
Habermas:

> Let's take the theory of individualization. In my usage individualiza-
> tion concerns the way that basic institutions like civil rights, education,
> and equal opportunities, produce and enforce individualization.
> Hence individualization is a basic social process and most people who
> are involved in this process – younger people, more educated people,
> those who are taking their *individual* rights seriously – even though
> they define themselves on the basis of those rights, are very sensitive
> to other individuals. This is a life-world matter. They live this way.
> Individualization means a special kind of social sensitivity and social
> reflexivity. In the traditional model, processes of secondary and
> tertiary socialization were at least partially unconscious because of the
> inertia of the old role models, but if those role models of man and
> women and parents and so on don't automatically work in the classical
> way any more, the rules have to be constantly re-interpreted. The
> work of defining and even inventing them on an everyday inter-
> personal level has actually become a necessary pre-condition for living
> a life in an individualized society.
>
> (Beck in Boyne 2001: 58–9)

Alongside risk proliferation and individualization, reflexive modernity is also characterized by an extension of politics. One of the root sources of this new and higher level of political energies is this phenomenon that Beck calls 'individualization', or, as Anthony Giddens puts it, the disembedding of social institutions. Work, family, education, healthcare, for example, are no longer as rooted in taken-for-granted and local contexts as they once were. This process is different from functional differentiation. It means that social institutions are becoming more abstract. They are subject to abstract measures of value, like money, points awarded in evaluation exercises, allocated scores in protocol-driven job interviews or contract tender competitions, relative positions on 'at-risk' registers. The forces that made western society into the modern industrial complex no longer exist in quite their original form; such distinctions as those between capital and labour, left and right politics, public and private, animate and inanimate 'are no longer correct or effective' (Beck 1997: 102). In these teeming circumstances, agencies previously thought to be outside or below politics 'appear on the stage of social design' (p. 103). Reflexive political life, the political life of risk society, as we have already seen, means that expertise has lost its privilege, its monopoly within the field of knowledge subject to permanent challenge. Decision processes – about airports, new roads, the administration of epidemics or the regeneration management of a whole urban area, to give just a few examples – are no longer able to be made automatically the province of a closed circle: demands for the multiple voices of the public come in from many points. The norms that such processes will follow are, Beck suggests, subject to discussion, negotiation and clarification. In one context, total consensus will be required; in another, a simple majority will do. This opening-up of decision-making processes, abandonment of closed discussions between experts and decision-makers, and self-legislation of processual norms (p. 122) is seen most clearly within the field of economic development, but the trends constitute a general promise, Beck's thinking suggests, throughout contemporary western society.

One example of such changes concerns what Beck (1997) calls the political bourgeois. It used to be the case that organizational decisions about corporate structure and policies, product range and investment strategy were arrived at by directors and approved by board members. This management group, which used to rule unchallenged, is now 'surrounded and permeated by alternatives

. . . It therefore becomes required to justify itself and dependent on negotiation, externally and internally, *vis-à-vis* the public (consumers) and the (current and potential) staff' (p. 127). It is no longer adequate for social organizations to try to apply the familiar rules. That was the mode of simple modernity. Now it is a question of intervening directly in the normative structure, to attempt by stealth, negotiation or force to alter the regulative framework. In this situation, passivity or ineptitude invites takeover and transformation. In corporate life, the structural forces of political economy have descended to the level of everyday behaviour.

It is not just the forces of steering, management and direction that have had to change and adapt with the arrival of reflexive modernity. The change has also impacted on the forces of resistance. Although Habermas's critique of Beck does not attend either to the accusations of technological determinism or to suggestions that the role of capital has been underemphasized, which have been levelled at Beck's work (Rustin 1994), what such critiques have shown is the importance, within the wider framework that locates Beck's work, of the politics of resistance. It is this area of countervailing force that Beck himself has come increasingly to focus upon, and which reveals that his perspective is (even though somewhat reluctantly) post-Marxist: a collection of theorizations in search of a set of global practices capable of being represented by organic intellectuals in a world redefining way.

If the strike was the definitive mechanism of resistance within simple modernity, such interference and destruction were typically undergirded by ideologies of advance and transcendence. Now the ideologies that inspire countervailing actions, to the extent that they exist at all, are narratives of reversal and return. Reflexive modernity is not just under siege from forces of *ressentiment* looking to turn back the clock. Its own internal condition is that of congestion: the blockage of roads, the flooding of borders, saturation of markets, violent competition for the same ground, viral contagion which follows the pyramid logic of every message creating at least two more. Beck does not engage with the fundamentalist war on 'the great Satan' of modernity (Bruce 2000: 16–39). His (self-evidently reflexive) concern is with what is happening inside modernity. The first prescription he had for the amelioration of congested worlds was 'self-restraint and self-abnegation, give up some monopolies and conquer others *temporarily*' (Beck 1997: 142). This pragmatic 'third way' approach, neither de-development nor free development, to the problems of risk society is probably his default mode. But there is a possibility for an emergent future-oriented ideology coming out of his recent thinking. It pertains to the thesis of cosmopolitanization:

> The nation state is a zombie category because it cannot handle the cosmopolitanization which has been taking place within the containers it labels. People now work internationally, they love internationally, they marry internationally, they bring up children internationally. These are everyday affairs. Sociologists have to find indicators for this, have to measure how far this reaches, and reveal the significance and implications of these everyday experiences . . . we need to focus upon cosmopolitanization and also its counter-trends, upon globalization from within the society and the forces set in reaction to it. I believe as Marx did with class, that cosmopolitanization is both a descriptive term and a political term. The analysis of cosmopolitanization as the process of nation state societies changing from within is both a way of describing how a society changes, and of exploring its political dynamic, of bringing to light the conflict between those forces which are open to change in a cosmopolitan direction and those which are closing up against it.
>
> (Beck in Boyne 2001: 47–8)

The emergence of hybrid identities, the almost physical power of immigration flows, the communications revolution that makes it possible to present images simultaneously to billions of people, could be some of the conditions which come together to make it possible for new world-level energies to emerge. Beck is unhappy at some of the variations this thought might take. It could lead to a romantic vision of a new universal class whose destiny is seen as creating the future, perhaps a cosmopolitan macro-subject, and Beck knows that millions have been sacrificed before in pursuit of such dreams. He does, however, edge towards such a picture.

Beck's future orientation is one of the main aspects of his work, and the final evidence for the validity of his thesis that risk society is qualitatively different from industrial modernity and may finally produce a cosmopolitan world order that has transcended the nation-state and will thereby provide a new framework for the reflexive treatment of technology, economic development and the distribution of both wealth and risk, is in the future.[3] Whether, however, there has been a historical rupture on this side of which is the qualitatively different risk society must be doubted. Unless and until a major set of causal dynamics for movement into a broadly predictable new future is identified, the links between the main processes of modernization and the near future will probably remain more important than the breaks.

Five theses on risk in the 21st century

1 It is the cultural context and the not risks themselves that explains whether and how we measure risks and whether and how we prioritize them

There is an infinite number of potential risks. None becomes consequential until identified in terms of its possible likelihood and the expected magnitude of its consequences. Once a risk is identified, it can be measured or estimated. If we know there are risks and we do not measure or estimate them, the explanation for that lies within the cultural context. When we do measure or estimate them, we have to decide the parameters of our concern, defining the tunnel through which we will see. The decision we make here comes out of the overall cultural context: its laws, customs, morals, tastes, standards of approved behaviour, and counter-cultural options. It did so with Bhopal and with *Challenger*, and continues to do so with base-jumping and barebacking. We do not have to formalize our decision-making, in which case we go along with the crowd, whether the roughly general standards within, for example, the international oil industry which did not conceive of the need to protect living quarters with blast walls on oil rigs until Piper Alpha in 1988, or the encouragement of friends who have taken these drugs before. What can succeed in widening or narrowing the decision-making focus in these cases is often hard to know, especially when viewed from outside the specific context.

The risks that concern us arise from our culture, from our knowledge, beliefs and interactions. No situated order of risk-priority will ultimately be capable of rational justification. But this does not mean it is useless to try to assess the costs and the benefits of a particular course of action. A definitive statement of what they will be may not be available, but in a context of significant responsibilities, like UCC's decision to transfer their Bhopal plant to UCIL, the analysis must be done. It is a matter of concern that one of the most influential bodies of cultural science thinking on risk should be based on a triple refusal of constructive engagement: with the attempts to model formally the structure of decision-making,[4] with the attempts to find out how people think that they might behave in particular risk contexts, and how people do behave in such contexts. In a small way, and somewhat perversely, this is evidence that the question of risk is ephemeral, contingent and merely a present form of cultural variation. Otherwise how could the anthropology of risk have been left defined by rejections of ethnography, comparative method, and interdisciplinary research?

2 The documentary and news media can at best only provide an introduction to the discussion of any specific risk

The *Challenger* case shows us that, to understand the different forces that affirm and challenge the parameters of risk analysis in any given case, there is no real substitute for detailed investigative social scientific inquiry. It is a source of real disappointment that investigative journalism is generally not going to come close to providing that. Even though the output of the documentary media can perform an excellent introductory service in relation to specific risks, it cannot be relied upon. The need to use emotive risk imagery to reproduce demand, and the lack of a recognized ideal standard, even if it is never met, within this crucial part of the public sphere, is disabling.

3 In any organization, risk-averse administrative systems can be balanced by entrepreneurial governance

It is possible that the administrative worldview may become dominant in a form that has emerged out of some sort of risk-consciousness. This could have the effect of a thoroughgoing cultural rupture. Whether the worldview becomes dominant, and if it were based on a form of risk sensitivity, may be two separate questions. It is too early to answer either of them. The anthropological evidence for cultural variation would indicate that, even if such dominance arises, in singular or duplex form, it could only be temporary and partial. However, the coincidence of Habermas and Castel on the characterization of administrative form is striking and deserves further thought. It is possible that an administrative society would be *ipso facto* a risk-averse society, but the drive towards entrepreneurial governance over the last decade (du Gay 2000: 1–14) might suggest that any link between administration and cautious procedure might be far from automatic. A debate between the Habermasian critique of systems and the ethnographers of the new enterprise culture bureaucracy has yet to really get going, but could yield important results.

4 Methods and techniques of decision-taking and risk assessment should form part of the formal curriculum for citizenship education

Contemporary western society requires its members to engage in continual selection processes: what to eat, what to wear, where to work, what to study, whom to see, and so on. Information about many of the choices that are made is plentiful. It is, however, intriguing that the processes of formal education do not provide any preparation – at least within the UK – for either group or individual decision-making. There are decision-making techniques. Not teaching individuals about the value of evidence or about decision matrices, or groups about strategies of compromise formation and committee management, does mean that the recipients of critical information – on amniocentesis, for example – may not be well placed to use it.[5] On the other hand, there is little doubt that these same recipients have been formed within a culture that has fostered through the visual media an appetite for risk, adventure and authenticity. Knowing that we might take a voluntary risk if on an adventure holiday which is one thousand times greater than we normally would, could mean some confusion about how to evaluate, for example, whether to go shoplifting or take drugs for the first time.

5 A key research frontier with respect to risk is at the junction of microeconomics, cognitive psychology and ethnography

What comes out of this inquiry is probably a shift of emphasis from the macrosociological, which is where the risk society thesis has its home terrain, to the microsociological, where there seem to be substantial opportunities for fruitful interdisciplinary work, especially between economists, cognitive psychologists and ethnographers. The question such collaboration might build towards is how, as individuals, we live with risk? At this point, we just do not know enough.

Notes

Chapter 1

1 The core components of most definitions of risk are an estimation of the probability of an adverse future event and the estimation of the magnitude of the foreseeable consequences should it happen. For further discussions of the definition of risk, see Adams (1995).

2 He was not alone in this thinking. Keynes made a similar distinction in his *Treatise on Probability* (published in the same year as Knight's book) and, as Geoff Hodgson (whose 2001 chapter is an excellent introduction to Knight) pointed out to me, it was critical to his General Theory.

3 In Karl Pearson's study of the Casino at Monte Carlo, he recorded that red came up 8053 times out of 16,019, which varies, as Gigerenzer *et al.* (1989: 269) point out, by only a quarter of one per cent from the 'expected' probability.

4 Although this would be a 'smaller' infinity than if we were wagering to win £10 on the first throw, £20 on the second, and so on.

5 See Descartes' (1985) single usage of the term *mathesis universalis* in his fourth 'Rule for the direction of the mind'. It is worth noting that Descartes himself thought that discipline and rigour could, in some sense, be separable from mathematical method and were necessary to a basic understanding of the 'extended' world (see Lachterman 1986).

6 See the Swiss Re Portal (established in 2000) at www.swissre.com, which is a comprehensive guide to reinsurance issues, provides a web-based platform (ELRiX) for electronic trading in risks (www.elrix.com) and gives insurance industry overviews on such affairs as major disasters (at the time of writing, the disaster of the moment was the collapse of the Petrobras oil rig off the coast of Brazil, and the Swiss Re site reported, only three days after the event, that its exposure was likely to be no more that 30 million Swiss francs).

7 The concept of the parametric decision-making context may be helpful.

Elster (1986) put it as follows: 'In a parametric decision, the agent faces external constraints that are in some sense given or parametric. First he estimates them as well as he can, and then he decides what to do' (p. 7). The question of which external constraints are parametric is only the starting point, since the question of the weighting to be given to each of the constraints will be critical. Additionally, such external factors may reduce risk to a decision-maker as well as increase it.

8 It is essential here to note that Knight (1921) did believe in both the theory and achievable reality of perfect competition.

9 In the eleven assumptions that Knight enumerates in his description of an economic system under conditions of perfect competition, there is no mention of extrinsic risk (except for a *ceteris paribus* assumption) (pp. 76–80). It needs emphasizing here that unanticipated consequences are not by definition taken into account in any decision process.

10 The situation is more complex when we look at Knight's work as a whole. Social policy and questions of history were central to his work. He was the English translator of Max Weber's *General Economic History*, was in regular contact with the Harvard sociologist Talcott Parsons, and became known in the 1930s for his analysis of the socialist economies.

11 At least outside the context of revolutionary systems of thought such as Marxism, anarchism and some forms of libertarianism.

12 Schumpeter's (1976: 132) thought, that the routinization of innovation may ultimately spell the end of the entrepreneurial function as production innovation, deserves re-examination on the basis of the entrepreneurial function redefined in terms of risk-taking in the global finance economy.

13 The treatment of risk within the framework of economic thought inescapably links to changes in the conditions of supply and demand that take place as risk is converted into phenomena of actual harm. Such changes are sometimes an extension of normal market conditions to such an extent that the market has often anticipated the conversion, and the actual arrival of damage may cause no abrupt economic transformation. A poor grape harvest begins to be economically anticipated with the first unusually cloudy weeks of the summer, and this process of economic anticipation continues with the arrival of heavier than usual showers in the early autumn. If markets are generally sensitive to risk in this fashion, they can be seen as risk thermostats (for an attempt to develop the notion of risk thermostat in a cognitive direction, see Adams 1995). To pursue this, we have to ask under what conditions will the price mechanism reflect knowledge of risk? The market as a risk thermostat reacts to anticipated fluctuations in demand, to shifts in needs, tastes and knowledge. It also reacts to movement on the supply side. What seems to be the case is that the market is a risk thermostat with an operating range defined by the estimated risks to the supply of

the wide but given array of services in play at any given time, and by the demand-related questions of need, taste and knowledge. The price of insurance constitutes a specialized risk-thermostatic sub-routine of the market economy.

14 There were elements of contradiction in consigning total responsibility for the Bhopal plant to UCIL, while having negotiated an exception to the provision under the Foreign Exchange and Regulation Act 1973 that Indian companies could only be owned up to 40 per cent from outside their country, and while requiring that every annual budget required approval from UCC (Bogard 1989: 28).

Chapter 2

1 The term 'media' is somewhat contested. Its general usage is, however, so well established that even double Pulitzer prize winning journalist Tim Weiner's view (1997: 7) that 'The "media" is what people hate . . . the "media" is a loathsome term that lumps together newspapers, television, advertising, movies and public relations, all of which are very different forms of the "media" ', is not quite sufficient to derail the term entirely.

2 Dictionary definitions of this term refer to instruction, warning, information, proof, evidence, actual people and real events.

3 The other main mechanisms for the dissemination of authenticated knowledge are education, the market, the professional/disciplinary associations, the library, the internet and word of mouth.

4 The situation is rather different in the UK where there is no constitutionally guaranteed right of free speech. London media lawyer Duncan Lamont (2001) notes that editors 'have long argued that the effect of our strict libel laws is to inhibit the media from giving the sort of information expected to be made public in America'. On the other hand, self-regulation in the UK is weaker than in the United States (Libson 2001; Mackenzie 2002; Wells and O'Carroll 2002); this has been demonstrated in a series of cases in the UK courts in which the recently allowed defence of 'qualified privilege', made responsibly and in good faith, has failed due to inadequate story-checking (McDermott 2002).

5 For a discussion of 'rational reconstruction' as methodology for theorizing in the social sciences, see Habermas (1973).

6 William Love had a scheme in the 1890s to build a canal system near Niagara Falls. It was never completed. Hooker Electrochemicals dumped around 25,000 tons of toxic chemicals, including over 7000 tons of benzene hexachloride and a substantial amount of dioxin (probably 30 times the amount that was released into the atmosphere in the 1976 Seveso explosion), into a half-mile length of excavated canal, between 1942 and 1953, although they did not formally own it until 1947. The property was transferred to the Niagara Falls Board of Education in

1953 with open admission that the site had been used as a chemical dump. By 1960, a school had been built over part of the site. By 1972, family homes were being built next to the site. From 1976, above-average rainfall raised the already high water table and led to chemical seepage, at which point investigation into local health records began. On 21 May 1980, President Carter declared that 710 families would be evacuated and relocated.

7 Mary Douglas (1999: 223) has three basic criticisms of the social amplification approach, which she defines through the metaphor of the intensification of signals emanating from 'stations'. First, the social or media amplification approach may tend to carry a political implication that risks are being presented as greater than they are. Second, the approach is naively realist in the sense that there is an assumed objective level of what the 'real' level of risk actually is. Third, what counts as the important signals from which 'stations' may be a fit subject for a research programme, but until that is well under way, the whole amplification approach remains under-researched and under-theorized. To these points should be added that the social amplification approach tends towards a bias in favour of reception/selection as the 'volume control'. However, a structural approach to the media at least raises the possibility that the amplification process is at least partially controlled at the broadcasting station. For an account of the social amplification approach that illustrates receptor bias, see Jaeger *et al.* (2001: 169–74).

8 Which may partially account for the occasional cases of plagiarism and fabrication that have been proved against investigative journalists. It is worth adding, however, that it is in the very nature of some forms of investigative journalism that stories are hard to check, and that the form is therefore open to abuse (see Daniel 2000).

9 Lest it be thought unreasonable to mention the 'blameless' victims of AIDS by blood transfusion in the same breath as those whose lifestyles were seen by some as the freely chosen cause of their afflictions, it is as well to remember that, for example, the emergence of AIDS only just succeeds – by a couple of years – the ending of legal sterilizations for the mentally subnormal in several countries around the world. We still live in societies in which, more frequently than we care to admit, having a weak or flawed physical constitution is seen as blameworthy in itself.

10 Another significant aspect of this case is the reproduction of an under-lying dominant ideology that being young, white and rich implies certain entitlements to health, wealth and happiness. The media nourishment of this underlying theme may create the impression that this equation and what it means for the general picture of social risk is largely unchallenged. Needless to say, this may not be the case. Michael Haneke (2000) explores this in *Code Inconnu*, especially in the contrast between the teenage Jean's rejection of French farm life with his father

(plus Anne's experience in the Métro, also featured in the trailer) and much of the rest of the film.

Chapter 3

1 She remains active in the field of risk, being a plenary speaker at the Brunel Conference on Anthropology and the Health of Populations in June 2002.
2 For a discussion of the formalist/structuralist tradition in anthropology, see Boyne (1996).
3 Or, indeed, in certain vectors, perhaps away from such systems that are already in place. Such could be the case with the controversy over the MMR vaccine in the UK in 2002, where social amplification of risk is transforming the image of associated health-workers into that of risk producers rather than risk reducers.
4 Just to push this point home, and in case this seems plain contrary to common sense, so that a list might seem quite feasible, and of course AIDS would be on it, right there towards the top, consider the following commentary on the Bergalis case. Belinda Mason, a journalist who became HIV-positive through a blood transfusion, wrote to President Bush, saying, 'if I was a young woman of colour in the Bronx, I wouldn't be standing up and talking AIDS. I'd be home worrying about how to pay the rent . . . I never felt that I was a member of an exclusive club that should go through life unscathed' (cited in Harrington 1997: 211).

It is also worth noting that the idea of the unprioritized list does not present a solution to the problem of how to make a list when there are competing criteria of priority. Not only is this because the identification of risk already arises out of a process of prioritization, it is also because the concept of an unclassified list is incoherent (and has been nicely parodied by, among others, Sartre with the character of the autodidact in *La Nausée*, Flaubert in *Bouvard et Pécuchet*, and Borges with the Chinese Encyclopaedia that Foucault cited in the preface to *The Order of Things*).
5 Since there is no possibility of establishing a single index of risk, of acceptable risk, for a society or social group, the contemporary risk problematic is postmodern, a problematic without metanarrative oversight (Lyotard 1984). It might be further noted that, according to Douglas (1999: 223), before 1986 there was no discernible literature on risk acceptability anyway.
6 To get further analytical purchase on those risks that are identified within the culture as being of immediate concern, Douglas and Wildavsky go inside the field of knowledge to practical questions of repair. In particular, they present Elster's distinction between strong and weak irreversibility. Strong irreversibility is where the consequences of action or inaction become clear only at the point when it

is too late to escape disaster; weak irreversibility obtains where consequences become clear and there remains some time to undo some or all
of the looming damage. Elster's formulation is elegant:

> Let us distinguish between two forms of irreversibility. For this purpose,
> it is useful to have the notion of a *frontier*, the value of some variable
> above which there are disastrous environmental or social effects. *Strong
> irreversibility* then obtains if (i) one can only know where the frontier is
> by hitting it, and (ii) it is impossible to back away from it when you hit it.
> *Weak irreversibility* obtains when condition (ii) is satisfied, but not con-
> dition (i) ... it may be the case that CO_2 effects are weakly irreversible,
> but they do not seem to be strongly irreversible. By contrast, a nuclear
> war is strongly irreversible.
>
> (Elster 1983: 206)

7 Douglas and Wildavsky show that the debate between scientists is
literally interminable. Among the factors responsible for that, the three
that they show relate to the inherent multi-interpretability of scientific
findings, to the circumstance that any piece of scientific investigation
can take a multitude of paths and can finish at a number of points, and
to the inherent weaknesses of the tools that scientists must use for
assessing risk.

8 A clear example of cost–benefit techniques at work can be found in
Pearce and Barbier's (2000) *Blueprint for a Sustainable Economy*. They
argue that the root structural cause of increasing environmental risk is
that we do not value such goods as air and biodiversity. The way to
value them is to put a price on these and other basic environmental 'free
goods'. When this is done, rational decisions can be made about such
things as a South American super-highway or a fifth terminal at
Heathrow Airport. The problem of this approach is that, as the example
of slavery shows, monetary evaluation is an invitation to buy to those
who can afford it and could, therefore, advance the global hyper-
development agenda. As we saw earlier, the calculative paradigm
routinely rules out of account levels and forms of consequences beyond
the immediate interests of the actors involved.

9 Douglas's more recent overview of these matters can be found in her
1997 publication, 'The depoliticization of risk' (pp. 218–30). Here she
says that national, internal politics has become more important, that
social scientists have tended to marginalize themselves, but that there is
increasing recognition of the importance of local understandings.

10 The power of radical environmental pressure groups was at its peak in
the 1970s. Maarten Hajer (1995) suggests that, as the nuclear issue lost
its impetus because fewer plants were commissioned, radical environmentalism faded with it. This did not mean that the environmental
agenda disappeared – far from it – but it did clear the way for the
development of a more technologically inclined, expert-minded and
policy-oriented environmental lobby. As Hajer puts it:

> The movement's emphases were no longer on alternatives for society, it started to focus on practical alternatives within society instead. Technology was no longer the focus of critique, but increasingly came to be seen as the discourse of solutions. A new type of knowledge became relevant. Activists . . . were now valued for various sorts of expertise (such as scientific or engineering know-how, or media, management or marketing skills).
>
> (Hajer 1995: 93)

In Hajer's view, there were four underlying reasons for these developments. First, periods of economic depression weakened the appeal of the radical environmentalists' critique. Second, the entry of scientists into environmental lobbying organizations weakened the critique. Third, new topics of environmental concern supplanted the nuclear issue, and these topics, such as acid rain, offered possibilities for expert-mediated compromise (on, for example, the reduction of emissions) that were just not available in the field of nuclear power. Fourth, the power of the environmental lobby was channelled by the activities of international think-tanks and policy institutes like the OECD (Organization for Economic Cooperation and Development), which, although powerfully critical of national governmental responses to environmental problems, did not provide the basis for the realization of the sectarian threat that Douglas and Wildavsky's analysis had foreseen. It seems now as if much of the activity with regard to environmental risk is taking place at the inter-governmental level, whether in terms of regulation collaboration (see Mol *et al.* 2000) or modelling competition (Parson and Ward 1998).

11 Just how dominant these categories are can be seen from the picture on the cover of *Thought Styles*, which Mary Douglas published in 1996. This shows four scenes: the isolated tree house, the stepped podium for the hierarchist, the tight entrance to the territory of the enclavist, and the route of the adventuring individualist headed upstream. These tableaux not only reinforce the importance of these categories here, but also help to focus the meaning of this category of the individualist.

12 Douglas (1999) argues that blaming is something close to a cultural universal: 'Insofar as a group of people is worthy of the name of community, blaming goes on as part of the normal political process (p. 228). It is, however, not always aimed in the direction one might expect. Looking to earlier societies, and examining what happens when someone dies, anthropologists have sometimes found that a moralistic explanation is given that places the blame on the dead person:

> she died because she had offended the ancestors, she had broken a taboo, she had sinned. Following this kind of explanation the action is expiatory; some purification rituals are called for. To avoid the same fate, the community is exhorted to obey the laws. If this is the dominant form of

explanation, the community which accepts it is organised very differently
from one that does not blame the victim.

(Douglas 1992a: 5)

Accounts of Bhopal demonstrate a quite complex interleaving of
meaning structures where the tendencies to blaming the victims wax
and wane.

13 It is perhaps symptomatic that, in his 1980s work on approaches to
mental illness, Castel emphasized practical eclecticism rather than an
earlier purism that came to feel outdated for him, describing the late
1960s and early 1970s context as one where 'il faut faire feu de tout bois'
(Castel 1982: 112). In the 1990s, he returned to being tougher-minded,
suggesting that metamorphosis completely changes the social landscape
and is by no means epiphenomenal (Castel 1995: 23).

14 A similar shift from liberal humanist treatment of the individual as a
coherent and ethically valued entity can be seen in debates within the
criminal justice system. As Mark Harris (1999: 7) commented about
pre-sentence reports: 'Offenders are no longer individuals to be re-
habilitated but risks to be managed' (I am grateful to Christopher
Boyne for this reference).

15 Compulsory sterilization continued in Sweden until 1976 and in North
Carolina until 1973. The rest of Scandinavia and 29 other US states
were involved in the practice throughout the three decades following
the end of the Second World War (Bates 1999).

16 Writing in 1995, Castel notes: 'The concrete circumstances which
underlie such notions as stability, precarious or lost jobs, involvement
in relationships, fragile support structures, or social isolation, are completely different now to what was the case in pre-industrial society or
the nineteenth century. They are even very different now from what
was the case just twenty years ago' (p. 21).

Chapter 4

1 Not all information; as we saw earlier, the very idea that all information
detailing all of the risks could be known or communicated is incoherent.
It is further worth noting that not all information that is relevant and
available can be accessed on demand: some of it may be held confiden-
tially, some may be channelled through a rationing system (e.g. wait-
listed appointments with experts), some may not be legally available at
all (e.g. medical advice on abortion in the Republic of Ireland) – the
point is that information, whether about risk or anything else, is not a
free good.

2 Some recent research suggests that framing may not have that strong an
effect in real world contexts (Edwards *et al.* 2001). Second, a related
phenomenon discussed by Tversky and Kahneman (1986) concerns the
independent framing of concurrent decisions. This is of particular

concern within complex organizations, since separate concurrent decisions may produce a set of results that would not be the preferred set if the decisions were framed together (see their discussion on 'The framing of acts': pp. 128–9) .

3 In terms of the parameters of the problem, compare this with the situation of 'the blinkered entrepreneur' in Chapter 1.

4 The 2002 Oscar-winning film *A Beautiful Mind* is based on the life of John Nash, the paranoid schizophrenic whose foundational game-theoretic work at Princeton and MIT is recognized in the naming of this basic equilibrium.

5 Slovic *et al.* (2000).

6 A high-profile argument from the US gay scene (Signorile 2001) featured the following statement from one of the protagonists: 'My HIV status: Poz. I prefer you to be: Poz'. That line was from a typical gay male profile (one of 31,627 as at 28 March 2002) to be found at bare-backcity.com, a site launched on 4 November 2000. In the 'About us' section of this free site, Steve and Kenny who run the site from their home in North Hills, California, have the following to say about the risk of HIV-AIDS infection from unprotected sex:

> What about it?? It will still exist if we have this site up or not. It's up to you (remember, you are an adult, aren't you) to decide how you want to run your life, who you want to fuck, whom you infect, and what you even believe. Also since you are an adult, you can decide to live this lifestyle or not, and accept the consequences for doing so. We are here for those who want to live this lifestyle, and don't feel that they fit into the 'safe-sex world'.

7 This is a position which is compatible with a view that cultural form will vary. We would expect on that view that the meaning of innocence would not be fixed. Although the category may retain a broad integrity in some contexts, as may be seen in the case of Kimberly Bergalis, this could provide the grounds for arguing that the notion stands in need of thorough deconstruction.

8 At least as measured by the resources and search engines of the American Sociological Association, the American Anthropology Association, the Cultural Studies Association of Australia and the various bibliographies held by Museum of Mankind at the British Museum.

9 John Grierson, often seen as the father of the documentary film, defined documentaries in 1925 as involving 'the creative treatment of actuality', and moving on from this crucial reference to creativity, Richard Barsam found there to be seven different types of non-fiction film. Just to give two examples, Dziga Vertov, the Russian cameraman who, in 1917, edited *Kino-Pravda*, wanted to re-present the images he made so as to show possibilities for a better world, while the ethnographic film-maker Jean Rouche filming in Africa in the 1950s sought a counter-colonial

cinema that would give voice and image to non-hegemonized local versions of the world. The complexity of the issues involved in the reportage of risk-taking deserves more serious attention than it has hitherto been accorded.

Chapter 5

1 There is not a rich variety of rigorous ethnographic studies of experts at work in contemporary society. See, however, Latour and Woolgar (1989), Traweek (1989), Kleinman (1995), Ahrens (1997), Knorr-Cetina (1999), Taylor and White (2000) and Law (2001).

2 For an extended discussion of Heidegger's critique of global technology, see Rockmore (1992).

3 See, for example, Pierre Bourdieu, *The State Nobility* (1998) and *Homo Academicus* (1988).

4 Post-Fordist developments identified by Piore and Sabel at the start of the 1980s centred upon the emergence of smaller-scale specialized firms with adaptable expert workforces. This dawning possibility of the expert on the production floor appears, however, to have rescinded a little as flexible production output is generally achieved through entry into the computer program, so ensuring that the next model on the line is the one required (Belussi and Garibaldo 2000). Additionally, it is worth noting that 'Any tendency to romanticize the high-performance workplace must be balanced against the intense self-monitoring and peer pressures that kept many workers effectively buckled into straitjackets of their own devising' (Knoke 2001: 203).

5 Areas that have not been mentioned relate to the developing reliance on technology in both commercial and domestic contexts, and to the computing and telecommunications revolutions. The former has given rise to the role of the technician or mechanic; the latter has witnessed the emergence of the help desk. Collapsing both cases together, it is clearly possible that technical support may be delivered by experts, but anecdotal evidence might suggest that this may not be the rule. The third area relates to the emergence of experts within the political arena. Cornelius Castoriadis (1997) is compelling in his arguments that experts in politics are an affront to democracy. He writes, 'The prevalent idea that there exist experts in politics, that is, specialists of the universal and technicians of the totality . . . contains the seeds of the growing divorce between the capacity to attain power and the capacity to govern – which plagues Western societies more and more' (p. 277).

6 Habermas (1987: 146) did, however, refer to the uncoupling of institutional systems from the lifeworld.

7 In the dialogue with Ulrich Beck and Scott Lash, Anthony Giddens suggests that the forms of trust within a society shift when that society becomes more risk-conscious (Beck *et al.* 1994: 186). That leads to a

situation in which what he calls 'active trust' becomes more important. This is 'trust that has to be energetically treated and sustained. It is at the origin of new forms of social solidarity today, in contexts ranging from intimate personal ties right through to global systems of inter-action' (p. 186). This is just a summative remark at the end of a dis-cussion, but it is worth noting that nearly ten years later Giddens' interlocuter, Ulrich Beck, can put very little more flesh on this line of thinking, saying that sociologists have to find examples of active trust, measure how far it goes and explain its significance (Beck in Boyne 2001: 47–8). Active trust is an attractive idea, but because it is agential, it has to be linked to powerful push or pull values and/or structures, and there is not yet much evidence that risk consciousness is producing these outside of social movements like environmentalism or identity politics.

8 Bruno Latour's perspective on how social agents grow in size and power relies on a similar achievement of taken-for-granted stability (see Boyne 2000a: 27).

9 A further consequence, slightly outside the main focus of this book but nevertheless worth mentioning, concerns the consequence of the trust deficit within the public realm for the cultural phenomenon which is called identity politics. Seligman argues that the consequences here of a public sphere that is hostile to trust has been the increasing sway of intolerant gender- and ethnic-related role ascriptions.

10 It might have been, although I am sure it was not, designed as a con-firming commentary on Castel's thesis of the metamorphosis of the individual from a metaphysical entity into an administrative construc-tion built from factors of risk.

11 The case of the consultant may be a significant exception to this sugges-tion of tension between management and expert functioning. Assuming the consultants are working to a clear brief, as experts their autonomy is restricted. As occasional contractors, the possibility of trust is limited. Their field of expertise as management consultants may be defended as real, but it is hard to see exactly how Castoriadis's challenge (see note 5 above) can be answered. The general rule is probably that their systemic function is to add legitimacy to the imperatives of manage-ment within a world defined by mistrust.

12 Still the priority in 2001 and the site of technological disappointment and multi-billion dollar funding crises. A reusable space vehicle was announced in 1999 only to be cancelled for lack of funds in 2001, already $900 million down the track. Art Stephenson, NASA space flight director said, 'Our technology has not yet advanced to the point that we can successfully develop a new reusable launch vehicle' (Hecht 2001).

13 Richard Feynman, a member of the Presidential Commission, com-mented: 'Engineering often cannot be done fast enough ... In these

situations, subtly, and often with apparently logical arguments, the criteria are altered ... They therefore fly in a relatively unsafe condition, with the chance of failure of the order of a percent ... Official management, on the other hand, claims to believe that the probability of failure is a thousand times less' (Feynman 1987).

14 Vaughan's reference to Thomas Kuhn here is explicit.

15 Sometimes the point where action has to be taken is after a disaster of major proportions. See (Chapter 3, note 6) Elster's notion of strong and weak irreversibility.

Chapter 6

1 Possibly the most obvious general characterization that deserves to be set alongside 'risk society' as a topic for discussion is 'surveillance society'. In just the same way that we want to ask whether the world is riskier now, we might also wish to know if we are being watched more than used to be the case. There is a close link between risk and surveillance, since a reasonable response to risk warnings is to set up systems of monitoring and surveillance. There is a story to be told of incremental surveillance by public and private organizations (see Boyne 2000b), but it is far from clear that it derives from risk-consciousness in a direct way. Additionally, the work that has been done in asking the question whether the term 'surveillance society' is an imaginatively fruitful beginning for theoretical macrosociology has not revealed what might be yet to come. Its impact may be especially at the microsociological level. As they explore what it is to watch people and be watched by them, social scientists will be able to assess the impact that this might have on individual expressions of risk-consciousness.

2 These three terms are generally interchangeable in Beck's work.

3 Bruno Latour pointed this out in an unpublished lecture in November 2000. In the same lecture, he preferred to use the term 'remodernization' over 'reflexive modernization', thinking the term 'reflexive' to be misleading. As I hope to have indicated, Beck's usage of the term 'reflexive' is crucial to an understanding of the way in which contemporary risk society differs from earlier modernity.

4 The repudiation of the rational action paradigm because of the lack of fit between its formal presuppositions and the 'real world' is, of course, a perfectly reasonable intellectual position to take. It is just a shade disconcerting when this is done from a position that does not fully address its own formal categories of transcendental subjectivity.

5 A formally inculcated appreciation of the value of evidence in making decisions in risk contexts might have produced a more apparently rational response to the MMR scare in the UK (see Calman 2002), but it would still require trust in the expert systems producing the evidence.

References

Ackerman, R. (2000) *Cutting Edge: Seconds to Impact*. London: Channel 4.

Adams, J. (1995) *Risk*. London: UCL Press.

Ahrens, T. (1997) Talking accounting: an ethnography of management knowledge in British and German brewers?, *Accounting, Organizations and Society*, 22(7): 617–37.

Anderson, A. (1997) *Media, Culture and the Environment*. London: UCL Press.

Armao, R. (2000) The history of investigative reporting, in M. Greenwald and J. Bernt (eds) *The Big Chill: Investigative Reporting in the Current Media Environment*. Ames, IA: Iowa State University Press.

Arrow, K.J. (1963) *Social Choice and Individual Values*, 2nd edn. New Haven, CT: Yale University Press.

Barry, B. (1973) *The Liberal Theory of Justice*. Oxford: Oxford University Press.

Bates, S. (1999) Sweden pays for grim past, *The Guardian*, 6 March.

Baylor, K. (1996) Biochemical studies on the toxicity of isocyanates, doctoral dissertation, University College, Cork.

Beck, U. (1992) *Risk Society*. London: Sage.

Beck, U. (1997) *The Reinvention of Politics: Rethinking Modernity in the Global Social Order*. Cambridge: Polity Press.

Beck, U. (2000) *The Brave New World of Work*. Cambridge: Polity Press.

Beck, U., Giddens, A. and Lash, S. (1994) *Reflexive Modernization*. Cambridge: Polity Press.

Belussi, F. and Garibaldo, F. (2000) Variety of pattern of the post-Fordist economy, in K. Grint (ed.) *Work and Society*. Oxford: Blackwell.

Bernt, J. and Greenwald, M. (2000) Enterprise and investigative reporting in metropolitan newspapers: 1980 and 1995 compared, in M. Greenwald and J. Bernt (eds) *The Big Chill: Investigative Reporting in the Current Media Environment*. Ames, IA: Iowa State University Press.

Bhargava, A. (1986) The Bhopal incident and Union Carbide: ramifications of an industrial accident, *Bulletin of Concerned Asian Scholars*, 18(4): 2–19.

Bogard, W. (1989) *The Bhopal Tragedy: Language, Logic and Politics in the Production of a Hazard*. San Francisco, CA: Westview Press.

Boseley, S. (2000) A fight for life, *The Guardian G2*, 30 June.

Bourdieu, P. (1988) *Homo Academicus*. Stanford, CA: Stanford University Press.

Bourdieu, P. (1998) *The State Nobility*. Stanford, CA: Stanford University Press.

Boyne, R. (1996) Structuralism, in B. Turner (ed.) *A Companion to Social Theory* (extended for 2nd edn, 2001). Oxford: Blackwell.

Boyne, R. (2000a) *Subject, Society and Culture*. London: Sage.

Boyne, R. (2000b) Post-panopticism, *Economy and Society*, 29(2): 285–307.

Boyne, R. (2001) Cosmopolis and risk: a conversation with Ulrich Beck, *Theory, Culture and Society*, 18(4): 47–63.

Brown, D. (1996) The 1990 Florida dental investigation, *Annals of Internal Medicine*, 124: 255–6.

Browning, J.B. (1993) *Union Carbide: Disaster at Bhopal*. Danbury, CT: Union Carbide Corporation.

Bruce, S. (2000) *Fundamentalism*. Cambridge: Polity Press.

Calman, K.C. (2002) 'Communication of risk: choice, consent and trust', *The Lancet*, 360: 166–8.

Carroll, R. (2002) 'Yes, prime minister', *Guardian Media*, 1 April.

Castel, R. (1982) *La gestion des risques*. Paris: Minuit.

Castel, R. (1991) From dangerousness to risk, in G. Burchell, C. Gordon and P. Miller (eds.) *The Foucault Effect*. Hemel Hempstead: Harvester Wheatsheaf.

Castel, R. (1995) *Les métamorphoses de la question sociale*. Paris: Gallimard.

Castoriadis, C. (1997) The Greek *polis* and the creation of democracy, in D.A. Curtis (ed.) *The Castoriadis Reader*. Oxford: Blackwell.

Chepesiuk, R., Howell, H. and Lee, E. (eds) (1997) *Raising Hell: Straight Talk with Investigative Journalists*. Jefferson, NC: McFarland & Co.

Cohen, A., Adoni, H. and Bantz, C. (1990) *Social Conflict and Television News*. London: Sage.

Cohen, S. (1972) *Folk Devils and Moral Panics*. London: Mac Gibbon and Kee.

Daniel, D.K. (2000) Best of times and worst of times: investigative reporting in post-Watergate America, in M. Greenwald and J. Bernt (eds) *The Big Chill: Investigative Reporting in the Current Media Environment*. Ames, IA: Iowa State University Press.

Daston, L. (1987) The domestication of risk: mathematical probability and insurance 1650–1830, in L. Krüger, L. Daston and M. Heidelberger (eds) *The Probabilistic Revolution, Vol. 1: Ideas in History*. Cambridge, MA: MIT Press.

Davis, M. (1998) *Ecology of Fear: Los Angeles and the Imagination of Disaster*. New York: Henry Holt.

Descartes, R. ([1628] 1985) *Rules for the Direction of the Mind*, in J. Cottingham, R. Stoothoff and D. Murdoch, *The Philosophical Writings of Descartes*, Vol. 1. Cambridge: Cambridge University Press.

Desrosières, A. (1998) *The Politics of Large Numbers*. Cambridge, MA: Harvard University Press.

Douglas, M. (1992a) *Risk and Blame*. London: Routledge.

Douglas, M. (1992b) The Self as risk-taker, in *Risk and Blame*. London: Routledge.

Douglas, M. (1996) *Thought Styles*. London: Sage.

Douglas, M. (1997) The depoliticization of risk, in M. Douglas (1999) *Implicit Meanings*, 2nd edn. London: Routledge.

Douglas, M. (1999) *Implicit Meanings*, 2nd edn. London: Routledge.

Douglas, M. and Wildavsky, A. (1982) *Risk and Culture: An Essay in the Selection of Technological and Environmental Dangers*. Berkeley, CA: University of California Press.

Du Gay, P. (2000) *In Praise of Bureaucracy*. London: Sage.

Edwards, A., Elwyn, G., Covey, J., Matthews, E. and Pill, R. (2001) Presenting risk information: a review of the effects of framing manipulations on patient outcomes, *Jounal of Health Communication*, 6(1): 61–82.

Elster, J. (1983) Risk, uncertainty and nuclear power, in *Explaining Technical Change*. Cambridge: Cambridge University Press.

Elster, J. (1986) Introduction, in J. Elster (ed.) *Rational Choice*. Oxford: Blackwell.

Ettema, J.S. and Glasser, T.L. (1998) *Custodians of Conscience: Investigative Journalism and Public Virtue*. New York: Columbia University Press.

Evans, H. (1998) *The Role and Responsibilities of the Media in the Twenty First Century*. Durham: Research Institute for the Study of Change, Durham University.

Evans-Pritchard, E.E. (1937) *Witchcraft, Oracles and Magic Among the Azande*. Oxford: Oxford University Press.

Fairclough, N. (1995) *Media Discourse*. London: Edward Arnold.

Fardon, R. (1999) *Mary Douglas*. London: Routledge.

Feynman, R.P. (1987) Personal observations on the reliability of the space shuttle: Feynman's appendiix to the *Rogers' Commission Report on the Space Shuttle Challenge Accident*. www.ralentz.com/old/space/feynmanreport.html

Fiennes, R. (2000) *Beyond the Limits*. Boston, MA: Little, Brown.

Flynn, J., Slovic, P. and Kunreuther, H. (eds) (2001) *Risk, Media and Stigma*. London: Earthscan.

Fukuyama, F. (1996) *Trust and Institutions: A Post-Election Analysis*. Arlington, VA: George Mason University.

Fuss, D. (1993) Monsters of perversion: Jeffrey Dahmer and *The Silence of the Lambs*, in M. Garber, J. Matlock and R. Walkowitz (eds) *Media Spectacles*. London: Routledge.

Garfinkel, H. (1963) A conception of and experiments with 'trust' as a condition of stable concerted actions, in O.J. Harvey (ed.) *Motivation and Social Interaction*. New York: Ronald Press.

Geertz, C. (1993) *The Interpretation of Cultures*. London: Fontana.

Giddens, A. (1991) *Modernity and Self-Identity*. Cambridge: Polity Press.

Gigerenzer, G., Swijtink, Z., Porter, T. *et al.* (1989) *The Empire of Chance*. Cambridge: Cambridge University Press.

Gollier, C. (2001) *The Economics of Risk and Time*. Cambridge, MA: MIT Press.

Habermas, J. (1973) A postscript to *Knowledge and Human Interests*, *Philosophy of the Social Sciences*, 3(2): 157–89.

Habermas, J. (1987) *The Theory of Communicative Action, Vol. 2: The Critique of Functionalist Reason*. Cambridge: Polity Press.

Habermas, J. (1992) *Postmetaphysical Thinking*. Cambridge: Polity Press.

Habermas, J. (1996) *Between Facts and Norms*. Cambridge: Polity Press.

Hajer, M.A. (1995) *The Politics of Environmental Discourse*. Oxford: Oxford University Press.

Haneke, M. (2000) *Code Inconnu*. Paris: Arte France Cinéma.

Harrington, S. (1997) Women and AIDS: bodily representations and political repurcussions, in D.S. Wilson and C.M. Laennec (eds) *Bodily Discursions: Gender, Representations, Technologies*. Albany, NY: State University of New York Press.

Harris, M. (1999) *Risk Assessments in Pre-sentence Reports: Their Impact on the Sentencing Process*. Cambridge: Cambridge University Institute of Criminology.

Harsanyi, J. (1977) *Rational Behavior and Bargaining Equilibrium in Games and Social Situations*. Cambridge: Cambridge University Press.

Harsanyi, J. (1982) Morality and the theory of rational behaviour, in A. Sen and B. Williams (eds) *Utilitarianism and Beyond*. Cambridge: Cambridge University Press.

Hattenstone, S. (1998) Sure, have an exclusive interview with our star actor, *The Guardian*, 21 August.

Hayward, S. (1996) *Key Concepts in Cinema Studies*. London: Routledge.

Hecht, J. (2001) Houston we have no money, *New Scientist*, 10 March: 4.

Heidegger, M. (1977) *The Question Concerning Technology and Other Essays*. New York: Harper & Row.

Herman, E. and McChesney, R. (2000) The global media, in D. Held and

A. McGrew (eds) *The Global Transformations Reader*. Cambridge: Polity Press.

Hodgson, G.M. (2001) Frank Knight as an institutional economist, in J.E. Biddle, J.B. Davis and S.G. Medema (eds) *Economics Broadly Considered: Essays in Honor of Warren J. Samuels*. London: Routledge.

Jaeger, C.C., Renn, O., Rosa, E.A. and Webler, T. (2001) *Risk, Uncertainty and Rational Action*. London: Earthscan.

Kasperson, L.B. (2000) *Anthony Giddens: Introduction to a Social Theorist*. Oxford: Blackwell.

Kasperson, R.E., Jhaveri, N. and Kasperson, J.X. (2001) Stigma and the social amplification of risk: toward a framework of analysis, in J. Flynn, P. Slovic and H. Kunreuther (eds) *Risk, Media and Stigma*. London: Earthscan.

Kennedy, S., Kuiken, T., Jepson, P.D. *et al.* (2000) Mass die off of Caspian seals caused by canine distemper virus, *Emerging Infectious Diseases*, 6(6): 637–9.

Kleinman, A. (1995) The new wave of ethnographies in medical anthropology, in *Writing at the Margin*. Berkeley, CA: University of California Press.

Knight, F.H. (1921) *Risk, Uncertainty and Profit*. Boston, MA: Houghton Mifflin.

Knoke, D. (2001) *Changing Organizations: Business Networks in the New Political Economy*. Boulder, CO: Westview Press.

Knorr-Cetina, K. (1999) *Epistemic Cultures*. Cambridge, MA: Harvard University Press.

Kurzman, D.A. (1987) *Killing Wind: Inside Union Carbide and the Bhopal Catastrophe*. New York: McGraw-Hill.

Lachterman, D. (1986) *Objectum purae matheseos*: mathematical construction and the passage from essence to existence, in A. O. Rorty (ed.) *Essays on Descartes' Meditations*. Berkeley, CA: University of California Press.

Lamont, D. (2001) Feeding frenzy, *The Guardian*, Media Supplement, 6 August.

Latour, B. and Woolgar, S. (1989) *Laboratory Life*. Beverly Hills, CA: Sage.

Law, J. (2001) Economics as interference, in P. du Gay and M. Pryke (eds) *Cultural Economy: Cultural Analysis and Commercial Life*. London: Sage.

Le Breton, D. (1991) *Passions du risque*. Paris: Métailié.

Le Breton, D. (1995) *La sociologie du risque*. Paris: PUF, Que sais-je?

Le Breton, D. (1997) Jeux symboliques avec la mort, *Religiologiques*, No. 16 (autumn).

le Carré, J. (1989) *The Russia House*. London: Hodder and Stoughton.

Libson, J. (2001) What is libel for?, *The Guardian*, Media Supplement, 26 March.

Lidskog, R. (2000) Scientific evidence or lay people's experience? On risk and trust with regard to modern environmental threat, in M.J. Cohen (ed.) *Risk in the Modern Age: Social Theory, Science and Environmental Decision-Making*. London: Macmillan.

Lomborg, B. (2001) *The Skeptical Environmentalist*. Cambridge: Cambridge University Press.

Luhmann, N. (1979) *Trust and Power*. New York: John Wiley.

Luhmann, N. (2000) *The Reality of the Mass Media*. Cambridge: Polity Press.

Lupton, D. (1999) *Risk*. London: Routledge.

Lyng, S. (1990) Edgework: a social psychological analysis of voluntary risk taking, *American Journal of Sociology*, 95(4): 851–86.

Lyotard, J.-F. (1984) *The Postmodern Condition*. Manchester: Manchester University Press

Mackenzie, K. (2002) Taking the chopper to the whoppers, *The Guardian Media*, 11 March.

Mazur, A. (1998a) *A Hazardous Inquiry: The Rashomon Effect at Love Canal*. Cambridge, MA: Harvard University Press.

Mazur, A. (1998b) Global environmental change in the news, *International Sociology*, 13(4): 457–72.

McDermott, J. (2002) To QP or not to QP, *The Guardian Media*, 7 January.

Milch, J.E. (1976) Feasible and prudent alternatives: airport development in the age of public protest, *Public Policy*, 24(1): 81–109.

Mol, A.P.J., Lauber, V. and Liefferink, D. (eds) (2000) *The Voluntary Approach to Environmental Policy*. Oxford: Oxford University Press.

Morehouse, W. and Subramaniam, M.A. (1986) *The Bhopal Tragedy: What Really Happened and What it Means for American Workers and Communities at Risk*. New York: Council on International and Public Affairs.

Morris, N. and Waisbord, S. (eds) (2001) *Media and Globalization: Why the State Matters*. Lanham: Rowman & Littlefield.

Nelkin, D. and Pollak, M. (1981) *The Atom Besieged*. Cambridge, MA: MIT Press.

Nohrstedt, S.A. and Ottosen, R. (2000) Summary and conclusion. Globalization and the Gulf conflict 1990–2000: challenges for war journalism in the new world order, in S.A. Nohrstedt and R. Ottosen (eds) *Journalism and the New World Order*. Göteborg: Nordicom.

Offe, C. (1992) Bindings, shackles, brakes: on self-limitation strategies, in A. Honneth, T. McCarthy, C. Offe and A. Wellmer (eds) *Cultural–Political Interventions in the Unfinished Project of Enlightenment*. Cambridge, MA: MIT Press.

Outhwaite, W. (1994) *Habermas: A Critical Introduction*. Cambridge: Polity Press.

Padgett, S. (1989) The party system, in G. Smith, W. Patterson and P. Merkl (eds) *Developments in West German Politics*. Durham, NC: Duke University Press.

Park, K. (1993) Kimberly Bergalis, AIDS, and the plague metaphor, in M. Garber, J. Matlock and R. Walkowitz (eds) *Media Spectacles*. London: Routledge.

Parson, E.A. and Ward, H. (1998) Games and simulations, in S. Raynor and E. Malone (eds) *Human Choice and Climate Change: Tools for Policy Analysis*. Columbus, OH: Battelle Press.

Pearce, D. and Barbier, E.B. (2000) *Blueprint for a Sustainable Economy*. London: Earthscan.

Pfeffer, I. (1956) *Insurance and Economic Theory*. Homewood, IL: Irwin.

Postman N. (1986) *Amusing Ourselves to Death*. London: Methuen.

Pratt, J. (1964) Risk aversion in the small and in the large, *Econometrica*, 32: 122–36.

Preminger, O. (1971) *Such Good Friends*. Los Angeles, CA: Paramount.

Rawls, J. (1971) *A Theory of Justice*. Oxford: Clarendon Press.

Robertson, R. (1995) Glocalization: time–space and homogeneity–heterogeneity, in M. Featherstone, S. Lash and R. Robertson (eds) *Global Modernities*. London: Sage.

Rockmore, T. (1992) *On Heidegger's Nazism and Philosophy*. Hemel Hempstead: Harvester Wheatsheaf.

Rockmore, T. (1995) *Heidegger and French Philosophy*. London: Routledge.

Rodrigue, C.M. (2001) Construction of hazard perception and activism on the internet, *Natural Hazards Research Working Papers*, No. 106. Boulder, CO: Institute of Behavioural Science, University of Colorado.

Rogers, W.P., Armstrong, N.A. and Acheson, D.C. (1986) *Report of the Presidential Commission on the Space Shuttle Challenger Accident* (five volumes). www.nasa.gov.

Rustin, M. (1994) Incomplete modernity: Ulrich Beck's *Risk Society, Radical Philosophy*, 67: 3–12.

Schneider, S.H. (2002) Hostile climate: on Bjorn Lomborg and climate change, *Gristmagazine.com*.

Schumpeter, J.A. ([1943] 1976) *Capitalism, Socialism and Democracy*. London: Allen & Unwin.

Seligman, A. (1997) *The Problem of Trust*. Princeton, NJ: Princeton University Press.

Shapiro, S.P. (1992) Libel lawyers as risk counsellors: pre-publication and pre-broadcast review and the social construction of news, in J.F. Short and L. Clarke (eds) *Organizations, Uncertainty and Risk*. Boulder, CO: Westview Press.

Shrivastava, P. (1992) *Bhopal: Anatomy of a Crisis*, 2nd edn. London: Paul Chapman.

Signorile, M. (2001) The contradictory faces of Andrew Sullivan, *LGNY*, No.162.

Simon, H.A. (1976) *Administrative Behaviour*. New York: Basic Books.

Slovic, P. (2000) *The Perception of Risk*. London: Earthscan.

Slovic, P. and Monahan, J. (1995) Probability, danger and coercion, *Law and Human Behaviour*, 19(1): 49–65.

Slovic, P. and Monahan, J. (2000) Postscript to 'Probability, danger and coercion', in P. Slovic (ed.) *The Perception of Risk*. London: Earthscan.

Slovic, P., Layman, M., Kraus, N. *et al.* (2001) Perceived risk, stigma and potential economic impacts of a high-level nuclear waste repository in Nevada, in J. Flynn, P. Slovic and H. Kunreuther (eds) *Risk, Media and Stigma*. London: Earthscan.

Slovic, P., Monahan, J. and MacGregor, D.G (2000) Violence, risk assessment and risk communication, *Law and Human Behaviour*, 24(3): 271–96.

Starr, C. (1969) Social benefit versus technological risk, *Science*, 165: 1232–8.

Steiner, H. (1987) *Moral Argument and Social Vision in the Courts*. Madison, WI: University of Wisconsin Press.

Strange, S. (1986) *Casino Capitalism*. Oxford: Blackwell.

Tabor, A., Philip, J., Madsen, M. *et al.* (1986) Randomised controlled trial of genetic amniocentesis in 4606 low-risk women, *The Lancet*, 1(8493): 1287–93.

Taylor, C. and White, S. (2000) *Practising Reflexivity in Health and Welfare: Making Knowledge*. Buckingham: Open University Press.

Tilly, C. (1992) Foreword, in J.F. Short and L. Clarke (eds) *Organizations, Uncertainty and Risk*. Boulder, CO: Westview Press.

Tonkiss, F. (2000) Trust, social capital and economy, in F. Tonkiss and A. Passey with N. Fenton and L. Hems (eds) *Trust and Civil Society*. London: Macmillan.

Traweek, S. (1989) *Beamtimes and Lifetimes: The World of High Energy Physics*. Cambridge, MA: Harvard University Press.

Tucker, K.H. (1998) *Anthony Giddens and Modern Social Theory*. London: Sage.

Tversky, A. and Kahneman, D. (1986) The framing of decisions and the psychology of choice, in J. Elster (ed.) *Rational Choice*. Oxford: Blackwell.

UNESCO (1978) *Declaration on Fundamental Principles Concerning the Contribution of the Mass Media to Strengthening Peace and International Understanding, to the Promotion of Human Rights and to Countering, Racialism, Apartheid and Incitement to War*. Paris: UNESCO (www.unesco.org).

van der Toorn, J.D. (1990) The seal epidemic in Europe and its consequences, *Soundings*, 15(1): 5.

Vaughan, D. (1996) *The Challenger Launch Decision: Risky Technology, Culture and Deviance at NASA*. Chicago, IL: University of Chicago Press.

Vidal, J. (1999) Call of the wild, *The Guardian G2*, 9 June.

Watney, S. (1988) The spectacle of AIDS, in D. Crimp (ed.) *AIDS: Cultural Analysis, Cultural Activism*. Cambridge, MA: MIT Press.

Weber, M. (1947) *The Theory of Social and Economic Organization*. New York: Free Press.

Weber, M. ([1904] 1949): 'Objectivity' in social science and social policy, in *The Methodology of the Social Sciences*, New York: Free Press.

Weiner, T. (1997) Digging for truth, in R. Chepesiuk, H. Howell and E. Lee (eds) *Raising Hell: Straight Talk with Investigative Journalists*. Jefferson, NC: McFarland & Co.

Wells, M. (2000) Sex on the edge, *The Guardian G2*, 14 March.

Wells, M. and O'Carroll, L. (2002) Beebie-jeebies, *The Guardian Media*, 11 March.

Wells, P. (1999) The documentary form: personal and social realities, in J. Nelmes (ed.) *An Introduction to Film Studies*, 2nd edn. London: Routledge.

Whittle, M.J. (2000) Amniocentesis, in *Green Tap Guidelines*. London: Royal College of Obstetricians and Gynaecologists.

Williams, Jr., C.A. and Heins, R.M. (1989) *Risk Management and Insurance*. Palatino, NY: McGraw-Hill.

Winch, S.P. (2000) Ethical challenges for investigative journalism, in M. Greenwald and J. Bernt (eds) *The Big Chill: Investigative Reporting in the Current Media Environment*. Ames, IA: Iowa State University Press.

Wittgenstein, L. (1980) *Remarks on the Philosophy of Psychology*, Vol. 2. Oxford: Blackwell.

Wynne, B. (1982) Institutional mythologies and dual societies in the management of risk, in H. Kunreuther and E. Ley (eds) *The Risk Analysis Controversy: An Institutional Perspective*. Berlin: Springer-Verlag.

Wynne, B. (1996) May the sheep safely graze? A reflexive view of the expert–lay knowledge divide, in S. Lash, B. Szerszynski and B. Wynne (eds) *Risk, Environment and Modernity*. London: Sage.

Index

ECONOMY, CULTURE AND SOCIETY
A SOCIOLOGICAL CRITIQUE OF NEO-LIBERALISM
Barry Smart

> . . . excellent . . . a probing survey of classical and contemporary
> social theory . . . extremely well written and organized . . . one of
> the best overviews of contemporary economy, culture and society
> I have read.
>
> Professor Douglas Kellner, UCLA

> . . . an authoritative analysis and a definitive defence of sociology
> as a critical theory of the market, politics and social institutions.
> A balanced and thorough critique of the neo-liberal revolution.
>
> Professor Bryan Turner, University of Cambridge

- How have economic processes and transformations been addressed
  within classical and contemporary social thought?

- What impact have the market system and market forces had on
  social life?

- How has the imbalance between the public and private sectors been
  felt in contemporary society?

Economic factors and processes are at the heart of contemporary social
and cultural life and this book is designed to refocus social theorizing to
reflect that fact. The author reinterprets the work of classical theorists
and, in the context of the move towards social regulation and protection
in the 19th and early 20th centuries, he discusses more recent transformations in capitalist economic life that have led to greater flexibility,
forms of disorganization, and a neo-liberal regeneration of the market
economy. As our lives have become subject to a process of commodifi-
cation, market forces have assumed an increasing prominence, and the
imbalance in resources between private and public sectors has been
aggravated. This illuminating text addresses these central concerns,
drawing on the work of key social and economic thinkers.

Contents
Sociological reason and economic life – No alternative? Capitalist econ-
omic life and the closing of the political universe – Cultures of production
and consumption – Without regard for persons: the market economy –
Affluence and squalor: the private and public sectors – Conclusion: new
economic conditions and their social and political consequences –
Further reading – References – Index.

c.192pp   0 335 20910 6 (Paperback)   0 335 20911 4 (Hardback)

GENDER AND SOCIAL THEORY

Mary Evans

- What is the most significant aspect of current literature on gender?

- How does this literature engage with social theory?

- How does the recognition of gender shift the central arguments of social theory?

We know that gender defines and shapes our lives. The question addressed by *Gender and Social Theory* is that of exactly how this process occurs, and what the social consequences, and the consequences for social theory, might be. The emergence of feminist theory has enriched our understanding of the impact of gender on our individual lives and the contemporary social sciences all recognize gender differentiation in the social world. The issue, however, which this book discusses is the more complex question of the extent to which social theory is significantly disrupted, disturbed or devalued by the fuller recognition of gender difference. We know that gender matters, but Mary Evans examines whether social theory is as blind to gender as is sometimes argued and considers the extent to which a greater awareness of gender truly shifts the concerns and conclusions of social theory. Written by an author with an international reputation, this is an invaluable text for students and an essential reference in the field.

Contents

Introduction – Enter women – The meaning of work – The world of intimacy – The gendered self – The real world – Now you see it, now you don't – Notes – Bibliography – Index.

c.160pp   0 335 20864 9 (Paperback)   0 335 20865 7 (Hardback)

FEMINISM

Jane Freedman

- What is the relevance of feminist thought to today's society?
- What do feminists mean by equality and difference?
- Can we find unity in feminist thought, or only conflict?

Feminism provides an introduction to some of the major debates within feminist theory and action. Focusing on the perennial question of equality and difference, the book examines the ways in which this has ben played out in different areas of feminist social and political theory. Jane Freedman adopts a refreshing approach by focusing on issues rather than schools of thought. Among the subjects she examines are politics and women's citizenship, paid and unpaid employment and the global economy, sexuality and power, and race and ethnicity. Finally, the book analyses the problem of essentialism for feminism and the challenge of postmodern and poststructuralist theories. Written in a jargon-free style, this book presents a clear aned concise introduction to a wide range of feminist thought.

Contents
Introduction: feminism or feminisms? – Equal or different? The perennial feminist problematic – Feminism and the political: the fight for women's citizenship – Employment and the global economy – Sexuality and power – Ethnicity and identity: the problem of essentialism and the postmodern challenge – Bibliography – Index.

112pp   0 335 20415 5 (Paperback)   0 335 20416 3 (Hardback)